MOTHER
TERESA
The Irish Connection

John Scally

MOTHER TERESA

The Irish Connection

POOLBEG

Published 2010
by Poolbeg Books Ltd.
123 Grange Hill, Baldoyle,
Dublin 13, Ireland
Email: poolbeg@poolbeg.com

A catalogue record for this book is available from the British Library.

ISBN 978-1-84223-441-9

Typeset by Patricia Hope in Sabon

Printed by
CPI Cox & Wyman, UK

www.poolbeg.com

Note on the author

A native of Roscommon, John Scally is the author of over twenty books, including the bestselling biographies of Dermot Earley, Tony Ward and Ger Loughnane.

Acknowledgements

I am grateful to a number of people who shared their experiences and reflections of Mother Teresa with me, including: Monsignor Niall Ahern, Cardinal Seán Brady, Ann-Marie Burke, Maggie Burns, Mick Byrne, Sr Claire Anne, Fr Brian D'Arcy, Katy Dobey, Gerald Evans OFM, Raphael Gallagher, Bishop Christy Jones, Mary Kennedy, Sr Stanislaus Kennedy, Sr Mary Killeen, Philip McKinley, Sr Teresa MacPaul, Fr Peter McVerry SJ, Bishop John Magee, Gay Mitchell MEP, Arnold O'Byrne, Gearóid O'Connaire OFM, Sr Damien O'Donoghue, John O'Mahony TD, John O'Shea, Dr Michael O'Sullivan SJ, Senator Feargal Quinn, Sir Cliff Richard, Kathy Sinnott, Caroline Swann, Gertie Shields, Archbishop Desmond Tutu, Bishop Willie Walsh, Tony Ward, Dick Warner, Gordon Wilson.

Sadly some of the people I spoke to down the years about Mother Teresa have passed on including Fr Seán Breen, Fr Michael Cleary, Dermot Earley, John McGahern, Jim Mitchell, John O'Donohue, Gordon Wilson and of course Mother Teresa herself.

Special thanks to the ever helpful Nigel Macmillan for technical assistance.

Thanks to both Micheal O'Siadhail and Bloodaxe Books for permission to use Micheal's poem "Hostel" taken from his collection Poems 1975-1995, Bloodaxe Books, 1999).

I am grateful to Brian Langan, Gaye Shortland, and all at Poolbeg Press for their interest in this project.

Contents

Introduction

It was the ultimate long shot.

In 1992 I wrote to Mother Teresa, more in hope than in confidence, seeking an interview with her. Months passed without me hearing anything and I had long since forgotten about the matter. Then out of the blue I received a letter with a postmark from India. I scratched my head and wondered who could possibly be writing to me from there. Munching my cornflakes as I opened the envelope I nearly fell off my chair when I read the following:

MISSIONARIES OF CHARITY
54A ACHARYA J CHANDRA BOSE ROAD
CALCUTTA 700016, INDIA
21st February, 1993

Dear John,

Thank you for your letter and for the magazine you enclosed. I am sure your article encouraged young people to grow in their appreciation and awareness of God's loving action in each unique life - which is so precious to Him. Works of peace are a sign that God is using you.

I will be in Dublin in May and you could contact our Sisters there and find out the dates of my stay.

Let the sunshine of God's love shine through you so as to bring joy and peace to all you meet and write for.

God bless you
M Teresa MC

1

After the interview, which took place in Dublin in 1993, I often contemplated writing a book on Mother Teresa's Irish connections, but every time I was ready to start, a new book about her appeared on the bookshelves which punctured my enthusiasm for the task. I did have a number of requests from publishers to write such a book after her death in 1997 but I felt that would be just cynical opportunism. However, with the approach of the centenary of her birth in August 2010 it seemed that the time was right to do so.

In her remarkable life Mother Teresa left an enduring imprint on the conscience and consciousness of the world because of her compassion and her work for the poor. Many elements of her story are familiar, such as winning the Nobel Prize for Peace in 1979, but I have always wondered why there was no systematic attempt to explore her Irish connections. Although most people are aware that a significant number of Irishwomen have joined her congregation, what is often forgotten is that when she chose to become a nun she joined an Irish order. She then began her life as a nun in Ireland. Throughout her life she had many further contacts and connections with Ireland. Even after her death her Irish connections remain as her Sisters continue work in each of the four provinces: in Dublin, Blarney, Sligo and Armagh.

When she first came to Ireland in 1928 Mother Teresa began a love affair with this country, an emotional attachment that continued right up to her death. This book tells the tale of a unique love story.

John Scally
July 2010

Chapter 1

A Day of Grace

Although I was at least a foot taller than Mother Teresa I felt totally dwarfed by her. Whatever this indefinable thing called presence is, she had it in abundance. Such was the force of her personality that even the briefest of meetings with her could be memorable. Early on a Saturday morning the sun threw long streaks of bloodlike red into her temporary Dublin residence. Although she was a frail, small woman she had the most marvellous eyes and perhaps it was this that gave her a presence disproportionate to her physique.

I have to confess I did feel a strong pang of jealousy when I met her. Her God was different to mine. She had stumbled on a God who dances and astonishes. The love of God had transported her, shattered her and consumed her like a fire. This was a passionate heart-battering God, the God who swept her up to the heights in a blaze of flame, whose face was full of the beauty of all creatures, of incredible power and glory. Such was the beauty of this God that we only partially taste its essence, like a dolphin dipping and plunging into the sea.

At one stage in the interview I asked her how she suffered personally and shared the sacrifice of Jesus on the cross. She pointed to my tape-recorder and said: "That and all that world." I could see that she approached dealings with the media in the same way I approached trips to the dentist. Glory and fame were anathema to her but although disconcerted by all the fuss she saw it as an opportunity to again spread the message about the poor. She believed in the wisdom of the Buddhist saying: "*When a finger points at the moon, only a fool looks at the finger.*" She saw herself as the finger and God's work with the poor as the moon. In many ways she was like an old-style missionary priest. With her the cause was every-thing and no opportunity for evangelisation could be squandered. Her zeal and conviction were awe-inspiring.

The interview had not been very revealing initially. When I asked her about her health problems and especially her "coronary incident" in 1983 she dismissed it with a wave of her hand: "St Peter must have said, 'Hold her back there. There are no slums in heaven.' I recovered, thanks to the goodness of God before the heart-attack actually started. I am more convinced of the work being His than I am convinced I am really alive." As if to reinforce the depth of her faith, when she was seriously ill she was offered painkillers but she refused them because she wanted to offer up her sufferings to God.

When I asked her how difficult it was to lose her forty-five-year-old father when she was just nine in 1919, she was not very forthcoming. I casually mentioned that I had some understanding of how she must have felt because my own father had died when he was thirty-five and I was just five. She seemed moved by that disclosure and the dynamic of the conversation changed dramatically and she was much less guarded from then on and appeared to be interested in me rather than the microphone.

The background to the interview had been the furore of controversy that had been unleashed by the revelation that Bishop Éamon Casey, an icon of Catholic Ireland, had fathered a child a number of years previously. I wondered if she had been shocked or upset by the news or if she felt the Church had been seriously damaged by the scandal it had created:

"Today what is happening on the surface of the church will pass. For Christ, the Church is the same, today, yesterday, and tomorrow. The Apostles went through the same feeling of fear and distrust, failure and disloyalty, and yet Christ did not scold them. I wish we could love as He did now.

"When I visited Assisi I went to the Church of San Damiano. Francis of Assisi had an encounter there [towards the end of 1205] which had a profound impact on him. The church was looked after by a poor priest who could not even afford to buy oil to light the lamp in front of a Byzantine image of the crucified Christ. Francis was captivated by this crucifix. It spoke to him: '*Go, Francis, and repair my house which, as you see, is falling into ruin.*' All of us must play our part in repairing God's house."

In her latter years and since her death, Mother Teresa has been the subject of some severe and penetrating criticism. Probably her best known critic is the writer Christopher Hitchens. In his 1995 book *The Missionary Position*, he posed the question whether this "wizened, shrivelled old lady, well stricken in years" represented "another chapter in a millennial story which stretches back to the superstitious childhood of our species, and which depends on the exploitation of the simple and the humble by the cunning and the single-minded".

I mentioned that in advance of her visit a prominent Irish journalist had criticised her because she was seeking charity for the people of the developing world – when what they need is justice – and that her charity was prompted by a desire to convert people to Catholicism. I was curious to hear if such criticism bothered her?

"If we were humble, nothing would change us – neither praise nor discouragement. If someone were to criticise us, we would not feel discouraged. If someone were to praise us, we would not feel proud.

"Prayer in action is love, and love in action is service. We need to try to give unconditionally whatever a person needs in the moment. My task is not to worry about why problems exist in the world – but to respond to people's needs. Some people criticise me because they tell me that if we give charity to others it will diminish the responsibility of governments towards the needy and the poor. I don't concern myself with this because governments seldom offer love. I simply do what I can do: the rest is not my business.

"We are Missionaries of Charity, and a missionary is a person who has to go and spread the good news. It makes no difference – today in India, tomorrow in Ireland, anywhere the voice of God calls you. Missionaries are people who are sent to become carriers of God's love. That's why we are called Missionaries of Charity. Someone once said to me, 'You are spoiling the poor by giving everything to them.' Then I said, 'Nobody has spoiled us more than God Himself.' He is also giving. He is total giving. Another person said to me: 'Why do you give them a fish to eat? Why don't you give them a rod to catch the fish?' So I replied, 'My people, when I pick them up they can't even stand. They are either sick or hungry. So I take them. Once they are all right, they don't come to me any more, for they can stand on their own.'

"There is no freedom if a person is not free to choose according to his or her conscience. I do convert people. I convert people to be better Hindus or better Buddhists or better Muslims or better Catholics. If I help people find God, it is up to them to find out what they want with Him. In our Constitution we say that 'The Missionaries of Charity will remain right on the ground by living Christ's concern for the poorest and lowliest."

Mother Teresa often betrayed her background as a teacher for nineteen years. She frequently illustrated her point with little stories.

"A Hindu man came to our Home for the Dying at a time when I was busy curing the wounds of a sick person. He watched me for a while in silence. Then he said, 'Since it gives you the strength to do what you do, I have no doubt that your religion has to be true.'

"I don't want the work to become a business. It must remain a work of love. Money, I never give it a thought. It always comes. I do not want money in the bank. I need money to use for my people. We do all our work for Our Lord. He must look after us. If He wants something done, He must provide us with the means. If He does not provide us with the means, then it shows that He does not want that particular work. I forget about it. It is better to serve than be served. This is His work, not mine. As long as we remain wedded to Him and our poverty, the work will prosper. I am not important. If people criticise me – so be it."

Amongst Women

I then moved on to tell her that many Irishwomen inside and outside the Catholic Church felt alienated by the institution's treatment of women. They felt that, while Pope John Paul II's *Mulieris Dignitatem* (The Dignity of Women) 1988 noted that one of the recommendations of the 1987 Synod of Bishops was for a "further study of the anthropological and theological bases that are needed in order to solve the problems connected with the meaning and dignity of being a woman and man", unfortunately that challenge had not been adequately taken up.

I then stated that many Catholic women echoed the type of sentiments expressed by the Irish President Mary Robinson in her inauguration speech in 1990: "As a woman, I want women who have felt themselves outside of history to be written back into history – in the words of Eavan Boland, 'finding a voice where they found a vision'."

So, did Mother Teresa feel that the Church was doing enough for women?

"When you talk about the Church – we all are the Church. We must not judge others but ourselves. We must remember that we will be judged on what we have done for the hungry Jesus, the homeless Jesus.

That's what we must always remember. A challenge for all women and men is to be a witness to gospel values in a world craving inspiration and guidance."

Mother Teresa was very emphatic in her response when I asked her if she was happy or if her work caused her frustration:

"We want the poor to be loved and feel loved. We cannot go to them with sad faces. God loves a cheerful giver. He gives most who gives with joy. Joy is prayer, joy is strength. Joy is love. Joy is a net of love by which you can catch souls. The best way to show your gratitude to God and the people is to accept everything with joy. A joyful heart is the normal result of a heart burning with love. Never let anything so fill you with sorrow as to make you forget the joy of Christ Risen.

"I have a happiness that no one can take from me. There has never been a doubt or any unhappiness. I do get angry sometimes. When I see waste, when the things that are wasted are what people need, things that could save them from dying. Frustrated? No, never.

"Sometimes I am sad. A woman came to us in Calcutta with a sick baby in her arms. We were going to do our best, and she gave me the little one. But the baby died right there in my arms. I saw that woman's face as she stood there, and I felt the way she did.

"There is a sort of miracle every day. There is not a day without some delicate attention of God, some sign of His love and care, like the time we ran out of food because of rains and flood. Just that time the schools closed in Calcutta and all the bread was given to us so that the people would not go hungry. For two days, our poor had bread, until they could eat no more. The greatest miracle is that God can work through nothings, small things like us. He uses us to do His work."

The Lord is My Shepherd

The dogmas of the quiet past are inadequate to the stormy present.

From the outset Mother Teresa publicly aligned herself with the poor and the outcasts. Like Jesus she formulated an alternative model of society. This Christ, exalted on the cross, healed the broken, fed the multitudes and significantly removed social stigmas (leprosy) and reintegrated outcasts like prostitutes and tax-collectors into society. The Church which Jesus called for and Mother Teresa tried to replicate, therefore, was a radical presence which empowered all people to have a meaningful life. A Christianity which is audible without being visible is a counter-sacrament. She sought to show that if Christianity is to retain its credibility it must forge a new alliance with the poor and marginalised. It must be bold enough to be baptised in the Jordan of the real state of people's experiences and climb the cross of poverty and social exclusion.

Accordingly, Mother Teresa had her own very particular understanding of Jesus:

"He is:

The Word made flesh.

The Bread of Life.

The Way – to be Walked.

The Joy – to be shared.

The Peace – to be given.

The Leper – to wash his wounds.

The Beggar – to give him a smile.

The Drunkard – to listen to him.

The Mentally Ill – to protect him.

The Little One – to embrace him.

The Blind – to lead him.

The Dumb – to speak for him.

The Crippled – to walk with him.

The Drug Addict – to befriend him.

The Prostitute – to remove from danger and befriend her.

The Prisoner – to be visited.

The Old – to be served."

Mother Teresa's understanding of Christ was forged on the basis of her own relationship with Him:

"To me:

Jesus is my God.

Jesus is my Spouse.

Jesus is my Life.

Jesus is my only Love.

Jesus is my All in All.

Jesus is my Everything."

Mother Teresa was not fazed when I asked her what it was like to be called "Mother of the World".

"I am just a pencil in the hands of the Lord. It is His work. We are called upon not to be successful but to be faithful. Holiness is for everyone. It is not for the special few but the simple duty of all. I have nothing myself. I think God is wanting to show His greatness by using nothingness. When I speak I speak in the name of Christ. Without Him I could do nothing.

"In the slums, I see Christ in the distressing disguise of the poor – in the broken bodies, in the children, in the dying. That is why his work becomes possible. I honestly believe that God is much closer to us than I ever would have thought possible. Not a day goes by without something extraordinary happening.

Always in our work we are motivated by the thought: *'There but for the grace of God go we.'"*

Honorary Irish?

Significantly Mother Teresa was not a fan of extensive rhetoric or grandiose vision statements or public pontificating. There is no need to preach the virtues when you live them. Perhaps one of her most powerful legacies to the Church today is to remind us that, in contemporary parlance, we should give a rest to talking the talk and channel all our energies into walking the walk. Her Christianity had a vital, personal quality rather than being something worn ostentatiously like a religious emblem. She helped in some small way to flower the salvation of humanity. She has managed to give a little hope to all she cared for and a little hope is a powerful and precious commodity.

The impression of visiting her was of a shaft of light illuminating the monstrous barbarism of poverty and injustice – a noble nature standing up for and with people she served and loved. Preserving that cherished image remains important for those who could see it at first hand. In fact, her testimony of faith struck not so much a note of hope as a symphony.

Leaving her, a verse I learned as a boy in school came back to me like an old friend:

Beautiful faces are they that wear
The light of a pleasant spirit there;
Beautiful hands are they that do
Deeds that are noble, good and true;
Beautiful feet are they that go
Swiftly to lighten another's woe.

Mother Teresa was aware of the high esteem she was held in by many people in Ireland. She had her own theory about the reasons for this:

"The Irish people understand suffering because of your history. Without our suffering our work would just be social work. If you accept suffering and offer it to God, those who accept it willingly, those who love deeply, those who offer themselves know its value.

"They know what I mean when I talk of doing little things with great love and that my message is simple even though it is not easy. Jesus wanted to help by sharing our life, our loneliness, our agony, our death. Only by being one with us has He redeemed us. We are allowed to do the same: all the desolation of the poor people, not only their material poverty, but their spiritual destitution, must be redeemed, and we must share it, for only by being one with them can we redeem them, that is by bringing God into their lives and bringing them to God.

"My advice to the people of Ireland is: love to pray. Prayer enlarges the heart until it is capable of containing God's gift of himself. Ask and seek, and your heart will grow big enough to receive him as your own."

Given her global status, I wondered if there was a particular space for Ireland in her affections:

"By blood and origin I am all Albanian. My citizenship is Indian. I am a Catholic nun. As to my calling, I belong to the whole world – and to Jesus. The people of the world are my people but I will always have a special place in my heart for Ireland."

Chapter 2

Heaven Knows No Frontiers

What human beings fear most of all is to make a new step, to speak a new word.

Change is the law of life, and those who look only to the past or the present are certain to miss the future.

JOHN F KENNEDY

Strands of Irishness are woven through the rich tapestry of the story of Mother Teresa.

When I examine that story I find that there is a wealth of adjectives used to describe her but a poverty of specific details about her personal life, especially in the early stages.

She was born Agnes Gonxha Bojaxhiu in Uskub

(Skopje) Albania, on August 26th, 1910, the youngest of three children. As "Gonxha" means "a flower bud" in Albanian, her mother called her "my little rosebud". Her sister Age was born in 1904 and her brother Lazar three years later in 1907. The story of the early life of the third child is the story of a bygone age when life moved at a gentler pace and there always seemed to be time for chat and laughter.

Uskub was a town with about 25,000 people which was then part of the Ottoman Empire. Contrary to widespread belief, Mother Teresa was born into a family of some comfort. Her father, Nikola Bojaxhiu, had his own construction business, building the first Skopje Theatre. He was something of a linguist who spoke Serbo-Croatian and Turkish in addition to his native Albanian. His prominence in the area was reflected in his membership of the Town Council, the only Catholic in this position. When I asked her where the myth that she was of peasant stock came from, she smiled: "I don't know but what does it matter? We're all peasants before God."

Her parents were an old-fashioned couple where the husband was expected to be the head of the family on whom responsibility for its survival depended, the provider who made all the key decisions. The wife owed, not obedience, but acceptance of his decisions. She stayed at home, had the children, looked after them and ran the house. The father was the custodian of order, the mother the catalyst of love and warmth. Mother Teresa remembered her father with undisguised affection.

"My father had a loving heart. He would never refuse the poor. We were very closely united after he died. I was very close to my mother. She was a very holy woman who taught us to love God and to love our neighbour. We called her *Nana Lake* – the mother of my soul."

Her mother, Drana, was one of those women who had a natural refinement and strength of character that no university education could provide. She had a deep devotion to the daily rosary. However, her mother was not just a pious woman. Her actions shaped her children's mindsets also. Part of her routine was to wash, feed and look after an alcoholic neighbour covered with sores. In addition she visited an old woman who had been abandoned by her family. She cleaned her house and gave her food. When her children became aware of this by accident, she told them: "Children, whenever you do some good to somebody, do it quietly, as if you were throwing a stone into the sea."

At one stage, when the family was about to eat their meal, a few poor people came begging. There was hardly enough food for lunch, but Nana Lake divided what they had in two and brought half of it to the gate and shared it out between the poor. She told her astonished children: "They are poor people. They are not our close friends either. Yet, they too are our brothers and sisters; they too are the children of God, Our Father. We shouldn't forget it."

On another occasion Agnes's mother brought home a basket of apples. She called the children to inspect them and they agreed that they were excellent apples. Then she put a rotten apple in the middle of them and closed the basket. A few days later she invited the children to examine the state of the apples. They found that all of the apples in the immediate vicinity of the rotten apple were also rotting and had to be thrown away. Then she remarked: "My children, you are good, thank God. However, the moment you come into contact with bad people, you too will begin to rot like these apples. Therefore, be careful about who you might mingle with."

Mother Teresa's father had been involved in politics. He was taken ill after travelling 160 miles to attend a political meeting designed to have the province of Kosovo, inhabited chiefly by Albanians, joined to a greater Albania after the First World War. The suspicion was, and remains, that he had been poisoned. The young Agnes was sent to get a priest and after the Last Rites were administered, her father was taken to the local hospital where no surgery could save him. Agnes remembered the demented ritual of farewell which followed with a steady stream of sympathisers coming and going like messengers from another world. Her mind blanked out many of the awful memories, subconsciously not wanting this forlorn image of her father to be her last.

On the day of the funeral every jeweller's shop in the city was closed as was the custom and the pupils in all the city's schools received commemorative handkerchiefs. The number of handkerchiefs given away was normally a clue to the riches of the deceased.

The funeral was a moving service; the priest hit a perfect chord and held it together with great skill and humanity. The grief, though intensely personal, was generously shared. The local community as always responded magnificently in times of adversity. Everyone rallied around. Every seat in the house was crammed with relatives and neighbours. At the funeral Mass the priest freely admitted that he had no answers to the questions that must be racing through the family's minds. The tears were for a life cut short, for the family, and for all the good Nikola could have done in the future. The entire family was devastated by the tragedy.

In the aftermath of Nikola's death, his business partner took the business and the family were left with nothing but their home.

Her husband's death posed particular problems for Drana.

Agnes saw her mother in three roles. There was the provider, often so immersed in work and the business of putting bread on the table that they hardly saw her for the whole day. There was the mother, putting on a show for her children in public and sparing them her private torment, anxious to give them the right impression, deflecting attention from the enormity of their financial problems to the trivial, using humour to avoid the pain, hiding her feelings even from herself. She continually saved the day with her warmth and optimism, displaying that maternal ability to avoid total despair by smoothing things over, not making a fuss, keeping the peace, preserving the family unit at great personal cost to herself. And there was the suffering woman, the moments when the mask slipped, and the heartache and grief became too much.

After a period of intense grief her mother set up her own business of handcrafted embroidery, later expanding it to include carpets. The practical needs of her family's survival dictated that Drana could not wallow in a dull fog of self-pity. For her children's sake she kept her own half-healed hurts as camouflaged as possible. Her children were the best palliative to the melancholy thoughts which engulfed her.

When I asked Mother Teresa to what extent she was like her mother, she paused before answering thoughtfully:

"I am sure in many ways. I learned from her that we ought not waste. One evening we were sitting around her, talking like children do for a long time. She got up and turned off the light, leaving us in the dark. She told us that it was not right to waste electricity on foolish talk."

Mother Teresa's desire for frugality and directing all available money to the poor almost led her into an interesting role in later life. She received a pass for free train travel on the Indian railways from the Indian Government and sought to get a similar pass for air travel. At one point she offered to work as an air hostess on her air journeys in return for such a pass. She clearly chose the wrong airline to approach because they turned her down. Had she approached Ryanair, Michael O'Leary would have jumped at the chance of a massive publicity coup.

Despite her strong spirituality Mother Teresa had a sharp business sense. When the Pope visited India, he presented her with his white ceremonial car as he left. She never went for a drive in it, but cleverly used it as the focal point for a raffle. The proceeds funded the leper colony she had been hoping to start for years.

The Call

I was naturally curious to find out how Mother Teresa had ended up becoming a nun as this was how the Irish connection was initially established:

"I was only twelve years old when I first felt the desire to become a nun. In 1925 we got a new Jesuit priest, Father Jambrenkovic. He started a branch of a society of the Sodality of the Blessed Virgin Mary. There we learned about the lives of saints and missionaries.

Father Jambrenkovic often told us about the Yugoslav Jesuits who went on a mission to the province of Bengal back in 1924. He used to give us the most beautiful descriptions about the experiences they had with the people, and especially the children in India. At that time some missionaries had gone to India from Yugoslavia. They told me that the Loreto nuns were doing work in Calcutta and other places.

"Between twelve and eighteen, I didn't want to become a nun. We were a happy family. But when I was eighteen, I decided to leave my home and become a nun, and since then, I have not regretted my decision.

"By then I realised my vocation was towards the poor. From then on, I have never had the least doubt of my decision. He," she points her finger towards Heaven, "made the choice. It was not easy for my mother to hear this news at first but when she thought and prayed about it she told me: 'Put your hand in His hand and walk all the way with Him.'"

Her brother Lazar, who was the man of the house following their father's death, was at that stage a lieutenant in the army but he was understandably a lot less keen on the idea of his family perhaps never seeing Agnes again. In response Agnes wrote to him: "You will serve a king of two million people. I shall serve the king of the world."

Significantly Agnes had already disagreed with Lazar over his attitude to Father Jambrenkovic's predecessor Father Zadrima, who had always demanded strict discipline and threatened the young with his walking stick. Lazar had been critical of him but his younger sister chided him: "It is your duty to love him and give him respect. He is Christ's priest." This revealed that from an early age Mother Teresa had an unquestioning acceptance of authority in the Church. This was to be seen often in her career – including, as we shall see, the most controversial aspect of her association with Ireland.

Mother Teresa was acutely aware of the cross that her mother had to carry when she had to say goodbye forever to the daughter she cherished.

"It was a big thing for her to give her child to God. It was a sacrifice. A sacrifice, to be real, must cost, must hurt, must empty ourselves. Sacrifice does not cause sadness, especially when you give it up to God. When you give to God there is a greater love as you dedicate your life to God through service of the poorest of the poor. The beautiful thing is that you give it to God and that is very important. Jesus said: 'If you want to give, be my disciple, take up the cross.'"

Her first call to a religious vocation was to an Irish missionary order. Why did a young woman from Albania pick an Irish order?

"From an early age I wanted to work in India. I picked the Loreto Sisters because they were well known for the missionary work, especially in India which always had a special appeal for me. They were Sisters who were with people in their suffering, sharing it with Christ. That was what St John and Our Blessed Mother were doing at the foot of the cross. The Loreto Sisters were an order who were dedicated to the hungry and the lonely, not only for food but for the Word of God; the thirsty and the ignorant, not only for water but also for knowledge, peace, truth, justice and love; the naked and the unloved, not only for clothes but also for human dignity; the unwanted and abandoned, not just for a house made of stone, but for a heart that understands, and above all a heart that loves."

As is the case with most religious, it was a big decision for Mother Teresa to turn her back on having a family:

"I saw it as dedicating my life to Christ, which allowed me to be more inflamed with love for God and His people. My Sisters and I are Spouses of Christ. We are all women who have the ability to make use of this love. I could not in conscience love a creature with the love of a woman for a man. I don't have the right to give that affection to any other creature but to God."

When she applied to the Loreto Order in Bengal she was told that she must first go to the Loreto Abbey in Rathfarnham in Dublin, where she needed to learn some English, before she could journey to India. On September 26th 1928 she left for Zagreb by train.

Because of the restrictions on travel imposed by the communist regime, it was the last time she ever saw her mother. In fact it would not be until 1991 that Mother Teresa returned for the first time to her native Albania when she opened a home in Tirana.

When I asked Mother Teresa about the sadness she must have felt, there was faint hesitation and a little nod but she did not seem to want to discuss the issue.

A Passage to India

The Loreto Sisters had a long connection with India. The order was founded as The Institute of the Blessed Virgin Mary in 1609 by an Englishwoman, Mary Ward; only later did the Irish branch become known as the Loreto Sisters. Mary was born in York in 1585 and predicted the apostolic influence of women in time to come in families, in public life, and in the Church. At the age of fifteen she was called into religious life. She went to enter a Poor Clare convent. Through special insights, God revealed to her when she was twenty-four that "some other thing" was destined for her and that she had a special calling. She went on to pioneer a new type of religious life for women in the creation of Catholic schools for girls. After she left the Poor Clares she worked in disguise to preserve the Catholic faith in England because of the restrictions imposed by the Reformation, notably the dissolution of the monasteries and convents. Then in 1609 she founded a community of active Sisters in Northern France. Unlike the cloistered Sisters in other convents, she and her companions educated young women, helped persecuted and imprisoned Catholics, and spread the word of God in places priests could not go. The Sisters lived and worked openly on the continent, but in England they had to work secretly because the law of the land forbade them to work in public.

Some of Mary Ward's ideas about religious life were viewed with suspicion because they were so revolutionary at the time. She developed three essential requirements of her Institute. The first and most critical was not to be enclosed. Next she sought government by a woman as general superior, something which bordered on heresy at the time. Finally she required flexibility in the hours of prayer. She was anxious that her Sisters would not face tension between attending prayers at set times and tending to those in need. Mary was imprisoned by Church officials who called her a dangerous heretic. In 1630, while she was imprisoned in a convent in Munich, Pope Urban VIII compared her Institution to "a weed in the cornfield". Her work was destroyed and her Sisters scattered. But she never lost hope and kept the flame burning. Even though she was precluded from active ministry she continued to live a life of prayer and sacrifice in service of the Lord. When she died in

1645 her Sisters were still suffering from a tainted reputation. Only in 1713 did Pope Benedict XIII agree to recognise the Institute, as long as it airbrushed out Mary Ward's name as founder. By 1953, though, the Vatican would describe her as *"this incomparable young woman whom England gave to the Church"*. In 2009 Pope Benedict declared her "venerable" – the first step to making her a saint.

In Ireland the founder of the Irish Branch of the Institute of the Blessed Virgin Mary was Frances Ball. She was born in Dublin on January 9th, 1794. At the age of nine she was sent to school at the Bar Convent, Institute of the Blessed Virgin Mary, in York. In 1814, Frances Ball was received into the Bar Convent novitiate at the request of Dr Daniel Murray, the Archbishop of Dublin, to be trained as a religious of the Institute of the Blessed Virgin Mary with the view to establishing a foundation in Ireland. There she received her religious training and made her profession in 1816, taking the name of Mary Teresa. In 1821 at the request of Dr Murray, she returned to Dublin with two novices to establish a convent and school there.

In 1822 she opened the first house of the Institute in Ireland, in Rathfarnham House. Built about one hundred years earlier the house was large and ornate, with a beautiful interior, polished mahogany and even in one room embossed leather wallpaper. A church was built in 1840, a novitiate in 1863 and shortly after a wing with a concert hall and a refectory.

As there were only three Sisters there, Teresa Ball decided to call the house "Loreto" after the village in Italy to where the Holy Family's house was said to have been miraculously transported. The name "Loreto House" was to be used for all the subsequent foundations that came from Ireland and resulted in the Sisters of the Irish Branch of the IBVM being popularly known as "Loreto Sisters".

The Loreto Sisters worked with oppressed, outcast and marginalised social groups. Reading their comments on poverty a century later, with the eyes of the third millennium (a risky business), it is striking the degree to which the Sisters reacted to the effects of poverty without apparently showing any concern for the system which caused people to be so poor and the total absence of demands for social reform. This was a reality in all female congregations at the time. There were a variety of factors which came together like converging lines to achieve this result. Firstly, Sisters were simply too busy with their apostolic work to engage in social analysis. Secondly, their position on the bottom rung of the Church's hierarchical ladder did not encourage them to be a critical, even a confident, voice. Thirdly, they were in part dependent on the social system for their position and property – it would not have served their short-term interests to be seen to be critical of the rich. A jocose comment from Mother Mary Aikenhead, foundress of the Sisters of Charity, to an aspiring Sister in the 1830s – "We are ignorant women, and do nothing but spin and obey" – may have had a much deeper truth than she intended. By entering convents, Sisters were indirectly identifying with a patriarchal power structure which severely limited their capacity to side with the poor in campaigns for social change.

Poverty was a big issue within religious institutes at the time. In 1840, in a letter to the bishop of Birmingham, Catherine McAuley, founder of the Sisters of Mercy, outlined her ideas on the ideal environment for the practice of poverty. The building should be "in the plainest style without any cornice". Twenty-five years later her congregation stated: *"In the parlours all that savours of worldliness should be carefully avoided, but neither should ostentatious poverty be displayed. The parlours are the parts of the convent most liable to secular criticism. Great neatness, with simple convent furnishing, will be most calculated to edify."* Excessive display of wealth provoked scandal. In 1873 when Presentation Sisters from Limerick settled near Melbourne, Sisters in convents nearby claimed that the house provided for them was "too grand".

In the Bible the question of where and how we can serve the Lord has an unambiguous answer. We find Him in the hungry, the thirsty, the stranger and the naked, we see Him wherever people are in need and cry out for help. The Christian God, revealed to humankind in a definitive way in the bruised and broken body of the suffering Jesus, continues to reveal himself wherever human suffering is to be found. From the beginning Loreto Sisters were women who recognised God in the course of their daily care of others. The heart of their ministry was the ongoing discovery of God's presence in the midst of the human struggle.

Although, as we have seen, their genesis came out of pain and division, their faith insulated them from the danger of being totally overwhelmed by their problems and ensured that the disappointments and disillusionments of their apostolate did not narrow their vision nor blind them to anything beyond their own problems. Although their apostolate brought them in a very concrete and immediate way in contact with great misery, they were able to see the face of a loving God even when nothing but darkness seemed present. In their practical "hands-on" approach to people in need they came in touch with a larger presence. Their care for the sick and the poor revealed the deep connections of their individual lives with the saving life of Jesus Christ. As they entered into the struggles and pains of the people they served in Ireland and beyond, they reached out to these people to reveal to them God's presence in their lives.

In 1834 the Loreto Sisters would answer the call for assistance from halfway across the world. A new and exciting chapter in the story of this group of women was about to unfold. In the mingled garden of weeds and flowers which is life this chapter too would provide a lot of challenges and call for many more acts of heroism.

In 1834 such was the state of the Catholic Church in Calcutta and Bengal that a group of Jesuits, including priests from Ireland and elsewhere moved there to take pastoral care of the area. This led to the opening of St Xavier's School which quickly attracted Muslim and Hindu boys as well as Christians. Its presence highlighted the need for a comparable school for girls.

In 1841 a German priest contacted the Loreto Sisters in Dublin, urging them to send a group of missionary Sisters to serve as teachers and tend to the welfare of the needy in Calcutta. Mother Teresa Ball met the priest but refused his request on the basis that the needs of the poor in Ireland had priority. However, the priest did not take no for an answer and indulged in moral blackmail, telling her that she might be responsible for the souls of the children she was denying a Christian education. Moved by his plea she allowed the priest to make his appeal directly to her community of Sisters. The community was keen on the project and as a result seven nuns and six postulants were chosen for the mission. On August 23rd, 1841, they left Ireland aboard the *Scotia* and did not arrive on the Indian shore until December 30th that year. The local bishop, Bishop Carew from Ireland, celebrated a Mass in their honour in the Cathedral of Our Lady of the Rosary in Calcutta. Just over a century later Mother Teresa would make her profession as a Missionary of Charity in the same cathedral.

The baker's dozen of young Irishwomen set up home at 5 Middleton Row and named it Loreto House. On January 10th, 1842, the Loreto Sisters opened their school. Such were the glowing reports from Calcutta that there was a constant supply of volunteers from Rathfarnham to India despite forty-two young Loreto Sisters coming to premature deaths over the next twenty years. Many of the Sisters did show the cumulative results of scarce resources, inadequate diet and demanding work schedules including seven-days-a-week rosters. However, their contribution was enormous. George Eliot's comment on Dorothea Brooke in *Middlemarch* could apply to many of these Irish Sisters in India and beyond: *"But the effect of her being on those around her was incalculably diffusive, for the growing good of the world is partly dependent on unhistoric acts; and that things are not so ill with you and me as they might have been, is half owing to the number who lived faithfully a hidden life, and rest in unvisited tombs."*

In the nineteenth century the Catholic Church was an important agent of social change, establishing schools, hospitals, asylums, temperance agencies for the purpose of "evangelising and civilising the poor". Throughout this period Irishwomen entered convents in great numbers.

Until the early seventeenth century the life of the woman religious was essentially one of contemplation and the cloister. This changed with the Counter-

Reformation when congregations of women religious were established to participate in more active works of charity, chiefly in teaching and nursing. With the formation of the Daughters of Charity by St Vincent de Paul in 1633 a trail was blazed for subsequent orders of women religious dedicated to the active apostolate. In Ireland the pioneer in this respect was Nano Nagle who was spurred on by the need to provide education for the poor.

Historical marginalisation was the fate of these women. One noteworthy feature of Irish historical records is that there is no central or even diocesan register of all the women who took religious vows in a particular period. In marked contrast all the regular and secular clergy in the country are listed on a diocesan basis in the Catholic directories of the time. Nuns were relegated to peripheral status – their contribution was valued to the extent to which they were of assistance to the clergy.

In the 1870s the famous Dominican preacher Thomas Burke undertook some publicity on behalf of the Catholic Church. He described the aspiring nuns as *"the high-minded, the highly-educated, the noblest and the best of the children of the Church . . . the young lady with all the prospects of the world glittering before her, with fortune and its enjoyments all around her."* It is most unlikely that the majority of women entering religious life were brought up with the silver spoon, whatever about being "high-minded and good".

Why did so many women enter religious life? A number of possible explanations present themselves. A desire to serve God and people in need was the main reason, but Catriona Clear in her acclaimed study *Nuns in Nineteenth Century Ireland* (1987) suggests a number of possible other reasons: a response to the evangelical "crusade" of the time; the search for personal and spiritual fulfilment; a more attractive alternative than married life; or an escape from particular problems and situations. A stereotype has developed of women fleeing the "real world" for the sanctuary of the convent. While that may have been true in some cases, it is equally true that religious life was arguably the only area in which the possibility of a career was open to talented Irishwomen.

In the nineteenth-century Irish nuns had in some respects a privileged, even powerful, position in society at large by virtue of their prestige and freedom to work solely on their apostolate without obligations to family or husband. This respect was hard-earned – the fruit of unremitting work, undemanding service, and passive acceptance of second-class status in the institutional church for both themselves and their ministry. In 1845 a contemporary observer described nuns as *"pious ladies who have forsaken all of the worldly pomp and grandeur for the sake of God."* In fact, while a religious Sister renounced rights over property and had opted to exclude herself from "social life", her social standing was higher than that of unmarried women and her scope of activity in a socially approved area was greater than that allowed to married women. However, in the Roman Catholic Church they were last among equals of those who took vows because they were denied any position of power in the institutional Church as a whole.

These nuns were remarkable women doing remarkable work in a difficult time. The tragedy is that their stories have never been told. So many heroic women's stories are woven almost anonymously in the tapestry of history even though they deserve individual recognition.

One of the curious features of modern history is that right up to the 1950s so many Irishwomen were ready, willing and able to leave the Emerald Isle to enter a convent in India, Australia, America or Africa. The willingness of so many women to enter religious life at a time of educational opportunities for women in Ireland has puzzled many historians. In his book, *The Irish Missionary Movement*, (Gill and MacMillan 1990), Edmund M Hogan contends that the exceptional impulse of sacrificial duty apparent in the leaders of the 1916 Irish rebellion carried over to subsequent generations and flowered most dramatically in Irish missionaries.

On a human level, leaving Ireland for India would have been a very traumatic experience for those Sisters, particularly because at the time they would not have expected to return to the country of their birth. Many of these Sisters had been fed on a diet of romantic nonsense about India, which bore no resemblance to the reality, to encourage them to join the Indian mission, such as what one overzealous novice mistress related to her charges: "If you want something to eat all you have to do is put your hand out the window and you can pick all kinds of exotic fruit off the trees." They left for the southern hemisphere with homilies ringing in their ears about the need to leave their will behind them if they were to be model, modest and obedient Sisters.

One young Sister who broke off a major romantic entanglement to enter the congregation totally misinterpreted the advice that she "must leave her will behind" in a heart-to-heart conversation with her novice mistress. Fully earnest, the Sister replied: "But, Mother, his name is not Will. It's Tommy!"

The Road to Rathfarnham

Mother Teresa's initial immersion into the Loreto Order came in a Dublin suburb:

"I was accompanied from Zagreb to Rathfarnham by Betine Kanjc who became Sister Mary Magdalena and she was my companion. My clearest memories are of Mother Borgia Irwin, who taught me English. She herself had spent many years as a missionary in India. I also recall the chapel and the community room. I was only there two months."

Between the lessons and as a reward for their improved proficiency in the language they were occasionally told stories about Ireland:

"Mostly she was teaching us about how to write and speak but there were times she told us about Ireland. I remember she told us about Saint Patrick. I liked his story and the way Ireland's great spiritual shepherd started life as a more humble one. He was entrusted with the burden of protecting his master's sheep from savage attacks by wild animals. Patrick began to feel that God was calling him for a special task. As he slept he had visions. Patrick was convinced that he was being prepared for a divine commission but he felt inadequate about conveying his spiritual experiences in words. A voice came to him telling him that when he would preach about Christ to others it was not he, Patrick, who was speaking the words but the Spirit of God speaking in him.

"I was interested that despite his great missionary activity Patrick also had a contemplative side. Before you speak, it is necessary for you to listen, for God speaks in the silence of the heart. He was a man of constant prayer. He wrote a famous prayer:

Christ be within me,
Christ be beside me,
Christ be behind me,
Christ be before me.

"Mother Borgia had a lot of stories about the first

Irish monks. One was about a monk [Saint Kevin] praying with outstretched hands for so long that a blackbird came to make a nest and lay an egg in one of them. They were very close to nature and she had many tales and legends about their love of animals. One story was about how three monks who were going on a pilgrimage to an isolated island, vowing to take nothing with them and to eat nothing only watercress. However, out of compassion for a fellow monk, they took his cat along. Once on the island the cat provided the monks with fresh salmon to eat every day. They saw God in the little, everyday things of life, particularly in nature. Little things are indeed little, but to be faithful in little things is a great thing.

"Although they had very little to offer they gave generously. They seemed to share the view of St Francis of Assisi: it is in giving that we receive. I especially recall St Brigid. I thought it was a beautiful thing that her monastery [in Kildare] was known as the City of the Poor, because of its reputation for hospitality, compassion and generosity. God loves a true faith in Him with a pure heart. Once, Brigid had embarked on a long journey and she stopped to rest by the wayside. A wealthy woman heard that she was in the locality and brought her a beautiful basket of apples. As soon as the apples appeared a group of people came by and begged for food. Immediately Brigid gave them the apples. Her giver was unhappy and said, 'I brought those apples for you, not for them.' Brigid replied, 'What's mine is theirs.'

"We also learned that the Irish monks earned a great reputation for copying manuscripts which led to such masterpieces as the *Book of Kells*. These monks teach us that we should have kindness in our faces, in our eyes, in our smiles, in the warmth of our greeting. Always have a cheerful smile. Don't only give your care, but give your heart as well."

Mother Teresa learned much less about Irish political history during her stay in Rathfarnham:

"I knew that Ireland had a long struggle with England and there was a lot of violence. Mother also told us about Ireland's famine. I remember one story she told us was about the Virgin Mary walking by a house in the West of Ireland on a stormy night. She and the Child Jesus had no coat to protect them from the elements. As they passed the house, the woman of the house called them inside and gave Mary a bowl of nettle soup, and an old sack to give extra cover to the child. Mary's final blessing was that the family line would always remain intact. They were one of the few families who survived the Great Hunger. A sign that God's favour rested on them was that their rooster did not crow 'cockadoodledoo' but rather cried out 'The Virgin's Son is risen!'"

My interview with Mother Teresa coincided with a major revival of interest in the ancient Irish Church and beyond, in what was known as "Celtic Spirituality". I wondered if she shared that interest.

"I would like to know more about it. I know that in this tradition a rainbow was understood as a love letter from God. I am told that the Celts were intoxicated with the love of God. They knew that you must give yourself fully to God. He will use you to accomplish great things on the condition that you believe much more in His love than in your weakness."

Retracing her Steps

There is very little documentary evidence available about Mother Teresa's time in Rathfarnham with the Loreto Sisters. My research brought me to a former archivist with the order, Sr Damien O'Donoghue. When she took her final vows Sr Damien headed to India in 1949, where she worked for the next fifty-one years and met Mother Teresa.

"All of the people who would have known her intimately in the Loreto have died. The consensus from everyone I've ever met in our order who knew Mother Teresa when she was with us was that she was a very nice, dedicated woman but that she never stood out. I often saw her around while I was in India and once I attended a meeting with our Mother Superior, Mother Teresa and a businessman and I was asked to take notes on the meeting. I saw with my own eyes at that meeting that she was a very good businesswoman but it is remarkable that everyone I have spoken to in the Loreto who knew her shares this opinion that she was noticeable for not being noticeable. That of course is a reflection of her humility."

In the middle of November 1928 Mother Teresa left Ireland with Betine Kanjc for the boat to Calcutta. On the boat they befriended three young Franciscan Sisters. On the way they went through the Suez Canal, The Red Sea and the Indian Ocean before arriving in the Bay of Bengal and landing in Calcutta on January 6th, 1929.

Sr Damien O'Donoghue has read a journal of that trip: "I became very friendly with Sr John Berchmans Joyce after I went to India myself and she had been on that trip with Mother Teresa and she wrote a diary of that long voyage. It was a remarkable document for a woman who was only eighteen at that time but there are no significant revelations in it. After Mother Teresa died and they were preparing the cause for her beatification they contacted me and read the diary but it really shed no further light on Mother Teresa. As she had become more famous down the years there were frequent requests for material on her. I had a very precious picture of her that was taken in 1946 and the BBC took it for use in one of their programmes and promised me faithfully that they would return it but they never did. Unfortunately we have precious little left from Mother Teresa's time with us in India and hardly anything other than her name in a record of postulants from her time in Ireland."

The Little Flower

Mother Teresa took her name in tribute to "The Little Flower", St Thérèse of Lisieux, and her "Little Way" of holiness. I mentioned this fact in passing to Bishop Desmond Tutu and he did not find her choice in the least surprising:

"I have a great devotion to Thérèse of Lisieux. In her whole life she fought for a 'higher way', a deeper intimacy with God and a faith that challenged others to put God first. As I am not part of the Catholic tradition I think my interest in her indicates that she has an ecumenical appeal.

"At the centre of her spirituality was prayer. CS Lewis is back in vogue now following the cinematic treatment of his *Chronicles of Narnia*. In his play *Shadowlands* Lewis wrote *'That's not why I pray, Harry. I pray because I can't help myself. I pray because I'm helpless. I pray because the need flows out of me all the time, waking and sleeping. It doesn't change God, it changes me.'*

"I think that is part of Thérèse's appeal to us

today. She encourages us to grasp the significance of retracting into oneself for inner peace, to seek solitude, silence and waiting, to be with God. It can't have been easy to reach such a prominent position in the Church at a time when women were often seen rather than heard."

When Agnes Gonxha took her first vows on May 24th, 1931, she took the name of Teresa to avoid confusion with a Sister Thérèse Breen, already a novice in the community. On May 14th 1937, Sister Teresa took lifetime vows of poverty, chastity, and obedience as a Loreto Sister in Darjeeling. For nineteen years, Sister Teresa lived the life of a Loreto nun.

In the 1930s and '40s poverty was endemic in Calcutta. As the political situation in India worsened in the run-up to its Independence, violence was common. Given her position as a teacher, Mother Teresa was shielded from much of the problem but she was determined to see it for herself, as she recalled to me: "We were not supposed to go out in the streets, but I went out anyway. Then I saw the bodies on the streets, stabbed, beaten lying there in strange positions in their dried blood. It was only then that I saw the scale of the suffering. When a poor person dies of hunger, it has not happened because God did not take care of him or her. It has happened because neither you nor I wanted to give that person what he or she needed."

The Call within the Call

As a Loreto nun Mother Teresa was a geography teacher. Legend has it that when she was asked about her understanding of educational psychology she remarked: "Make sure to get the pupil outside the classroom before they wet the floor!"

By all accounts her talent as a teacher was that she was able to communicate and transmit her passion to her pupils and to awaken their creativity and take them on a magical journey of imaginative exploration, even if at times she took them on side-tracks because of the complexity of her language and the density and depth of her thought.

Her pupils needed a hero or heroine and her flair was to inspire them with a different vision of life's possibilities. In the cloistered atmosphere of their stuffy classroom, their retiring teenage sensibilities were exposed to the full vigour of her powerful personality. Her eyes sparkled, almost flashed, as ideas and indignation energised her mind. Her most frequent complaint was about the almost total lack of imagination in the classroom and the fact her pupils were living in a fog of uncertainty and ignorance. However, after nineteen years as a Geography teacher she turned her back on that path to live the geography of compassion:

"In 1946 I was going to Darjeeling, to make my retreat. It was in that train I heard the call to give up all and follow Him into the slums to serve Him among the poorest of the poor. I knew that it was His will, and that I had to follow Him. There was no doubt that it was going to be His work. In Matthew 25 Jesus gave us the test for the way to follow him: 'I was hungry and you fed me. I was thirsty and you gave me to drink. I was in prison and you visited me.' I had never believed though that passage was meant to apply to me – but all of a sudden it did. I heard the call to give up and follow Christ into the slums to serve Him among the poorest of the poor. It was an order. I was to leave the convent and help the poor while living among them. I wanted to be a missionary. I wanted to go out and live the life of Christ with the people."

On a purely human level this was going to be difficult for her:

"I love teaching most of all so it was hard to leave that behind."

There was also a major bureaucratic challenge:

"I had first to apply to the Archbishop of Calcutta. Then with the approval of the Mother General of the Loreto Order I had permission to write to Rome. I wrote to the Holy Father, Pope Pius XII. I told him that I had a vocation, that God was calling me to give up all and to surrender myself to Him in the service of the poorest of the poor in the slums."

The Loreto Sisters helped Mother Teresa in a

practical way to establish her fledging order, with her young Sisters receiving free education at Loreto schools, something which Mother Teresa never forgot.

When I spoke to Sr Damien O'Donoghue I wondered though if there had been any residual resentment on the part of the Loretos at Mother Teresa's decision to leave:

"I went to India the year after she left the Loreto. It was a great time to arrive because India had just got its Independence and there were such great hopes and plans for the country and people were in such good spirits and with people like Mr Nehru in charge the country seemed to have the leaders to guide the country towards a bright new dawn. I saw at first hand how friendly Mother Teresa was with our Sisters. We saw her around a lot. She was always cheerful with us and she always said that she never left us but had a vocation within a vocation. I thought of those words when she died. There was great mourning when she died in India as a whole. Her funeral Mass was celebrated in St Thomas's Church which is practically in our grounds at Loreto House. I thought it was very symbolic that she had come back to us at the end of her life, when she had started off on her journey with us."

Mother Teresa told me about her own thoughts on the transition:

"Abandoning Loreto was an even harder sacrifice for me than leaving my family that first time in order to follow my vocation. But I had to do it. It was a calling. I knew where I had to go; I did not know how to get there. In my heart I remain a Loreto."

On August 8th 1948 Mother Teresa laid aside the Loreto habit and clothed herself in the white sari, with a blue border and cross on the shoulder. She had five rupees in her pocket when she left to establish the Missionaries of Charity: "I left the Loreto convent and I went first to the Loreto Sisters in Patna to get some training in medical care so that I might enter the houses of the poor and see the children and the sick."

Those caring medical staff helped her to see the healing hands of Jesus in human form; they were people who had the empathy and understanding that the perilous emotional and physical condition of their patients craved for. They saw the need not just to cater for people's physiological needs, but also for their emotional and psychological needs as well.

Then the time came when she had to leave Patna as well:

"Our Lord wanted me to be a free nun, covered with the poverty of the cross. But I learned a great lesson after I left the Loreto. When looking for a home I walked and walked until my legs and arms ached. I thought how much they [the poor] must ache in soul and body looking for a home, food and health. Then the comfort of Loreto came to tempt me, but of my own free choice, and out of love for

Him, I desired to remain and do whatever be His holy will in my regard."

Another Irish connection came into play when Mother Teresa was offered a place of her own by Michael Gomes, an Indian Catholic, at 14 Creek Lane in Calcutta. He refused to take any money from Mother Teresa because he was an active member of the Legion of Mary, an association of lay people who serve the Church on a voluntary basis, founded in Dublin by Frank Duff. For Gomes, Mother Teresa was a blessing from God. He described her presence: "We received. We did not give."

Although she had no resources, her ammunition was a fierce determination. She was not a woman to take no for an answer. One day she went to a pharmacy with a long list of medicines and the pharmacist told her he could not possibly help. However, she was undaunted and sat down and recited her rosary. Finally, as her sit-in persisted, the pharmacist took another look at her list and ended up giving her all the medicines she wanted.

Soon she was joined by novices, mainly girls she had taught in school, and her work spread. Her own convictions reflected from her into her community like a stone thrown into a pool of water: one good action set off another.

She did not spend much time thinking about the name for her new congregation: "Missionaries of

Charity – in other words, messengers of God's love to the outskirts. The people don't see us doing anything else. In determining which work would be done, there was no planning at all. I headed the work in accordance to how I felt called by the people's sufferings. God made me see what He wanted me to do."

The Table of the Lord

Mother Teresa is a name synonymous with care for the poor and sick. However, there was much more to her activities than bandaging the wounds of society and stirring the conscience of the people of India. She sought to resolve the Martha-Mary tension of the Gospel by seeking a harmonious balance between activity and contemplation. She and her Sisters were ever ready when necessity knocked at their door; for their only watchword was "duty" – duty to God – duty to their neighbour, and "neighbour" with them meant every class and sect in society.

At the altar of the Motherhouse chapel was a large crucifix with two words: "*I THIRST*". These words have a dual significance. They recall the words of Jesus on the cross. They also recall his thirst for the love of humankind.

All share the gospel call: "*Seek ye first the kingdom of God.*" As the Sisters were increasingly involved in different apostolates, the Eucharist provided Mother Teresa with a common basis for the different approaches to their search for the kingdom, nurturing a sense of community and solidarity.

From its earliest days the Christian community has gathered to celebrate the Eucharist. There are two crucial dimensions to the Eucharist: thanksgiving and remembrance. In the Eucharistic celebration Christians have always found their identity – thanking God and remembering how God revealed the divine plan for our salvation in the life, death and resurrection of Jesus. The Eucharist is the primary occasion of Christian self-understanding:

"To those who say they admire my courage, I have to tell them that I would not have any if I were not convinced that each time I touch the body of a leper, a body that reeks with a foul stench, I touch Christ's body, the same Christ I receive in the Eucharist. The Mass is the spiritual food that sustains me. I could not pass a single day or hour in my life without it. In the Eucharist, I see Christ in the appearance of bread."

It may be that the most important legacy of Mother Teresa to the Missionaries of Charity today is a reminder of the centrality of the Eucharist in their lives. She knew that this was an important insight because of the danger of Sisters becoming too preoccupied with the apostolate. Should they limit themselves to finding Christ's image in the people they served, they would be limiting themselves to contemplating the works of the Lord without being able to contemplate the Lord Himself:

"Without Him we could do nothing. It is at the altar that we meet our suffering poor. In Him we see that suffering can become a means to greater love, and greater generosity."

In the Name of the Son

From the very beginning Mother Teresa's Sisters were women who thought, spoke and acted not in their own name but in the name of the Lord. From the outset Mother Teresa's Sisters showed a great tenderness and an explicit recognition that they were part of a healing ministry, that Jesus Christ was to be encountered in the suffering of the sick and that the order was founded for the poor and the marginalised. A Missionary of Charity Sister was one who lived in communion with Jesus, and through Him in the Trinitarian God. To be true to the gospel vision it is necessary to keep one's eyes on the Lord, to remain attentive to His will and to listen with care to His voice (Lk 10:42). Only with, in and through Jesus Christ can the apostolate bear fruit. Consequently the first, indeed in a sense the only concern must be to live in ongoing communion with the One who calls us out to witness in His name.

From this starting point it was inevitable that Mother Teresa would recognise that prayer was the basis and centre of all ministry. The Sister of Mother Teresa must be first and foremost a woman of prayer. Without prayer, religious life easily descends to a mere busy life in which a person's need for respect or affection dominates actions and being busy becomes a badge of honour, an end in itself. It is not necessarily true that absence makes the heart grow fonder. As many a ruined romance has demonstrated, absence may cause the heart to wander. The parallel for prayer life does not need to be laboured.

While the founding Sisters in many cases heroically gave all of themselves to the apostolate, they never deluded themselves that their work was their prayer.

Today the question is posed: "Who ministers to the minister?" Mother Teresa recognised that healthy ministry was impossible unless her Sisters first of all ministered to each other. Like everybody else, Sisters are broken and fragile people. They can only care for the wounds of others if they allow their own wounds to be healed by those who live with them in community, aspiring to a quality of life and ministry which attempts to give renewed heart to the Christian life by a radical commitment to simplicity, sharing and intimacy.

"The practice of faith is very real. It's very natural for our Sisters to talk about God and what He means to them. I can't solve all the problems but I can do a little. The people say thanks for walking with us. They don't praise me for great sermons but they appreciate that I'm there for them.

"Today countries are concentrating too much on means to defend their borders. Yet those countries know so little about the poverty and suffering that makes the human beings who live inside such borders feel so lonely. If instead they would worry about giving these defenceless beings some food, some shelter, some healthcare, some clothes, it is undeniable that the world would be a more peaceful and happy place to live.

"Poverty has not been created by God. We are the ones who have created poverty. Before God, we are all poor. Jesus is the one we take care of, visit, clothe, feed and comfort every time we do this to the poorest of the poor, to the sick, to the dying, to the lepers, and to the ones who suffer from AIDS. We should not serve the poor like they were Jesus. We should serve the poor because they are Jesus. The poor anywhere in the world are Christ who suffers. In them, the Son of God lives and dies. Through them, God shows his face. We have refused to be instruments of love in the hands of God to give the poor a piece of bread, to offer them a dress with which to ward off the cold. It has happened because we did not recognise Christ when, once more, he appeared under the guise of pain, identified with a man numb from the cold, dying of hunger, when he came in a lonely human being, in a lost child in search of a home.

"To be happy with God on earth presupposes certain things: to love the way he loves; to help the way he helps; to give the way he gives; to save the way he saves; to remain in his presence twenty-four hours a day; to touch him in the poor and in those who suffer. When we touch the sick and needy, we touch the suffering of Christ. I pay no attention to numbers; what matters is the people. I rely on one. There is only one: Jesus."

One of Mother Teresa's priorities was to set up a home for the dying called *Nirmal Hriday* (Home of the Pure Heart). If in life people could not live in dignity then she believed that in their last hours on this earth they could be treated with respect and care. Apart from human concern for the sick she had a very strong sense that they should be treated with dignity and with Christian-inspired compassion.

"The first woman I saw, I myself picked up from the street. She had been half eaten by the rats and ants. I took her to the hospital but they could not do anything for her. They only took her in because I refused to move until they accepted her. From there I went to the authorities and I asked them to give me a place where I could bring these people because on the same day I found other people dying in the streets. The health officer of the municipality took me to the

Hindu temple and gave me an empty building beside it. Within twenty-four hours we had our patients there and we started the work of the home for the sick and dying who are destitute."

In 1949 Mother Teresa applied for and was granted Indian citizenship. However, her love affair with Ireland would continue for the rest of her life in a number of different ways.

Chapter 3

Ireland's Call

Conscious of Mother Teresa's early exposure to Ireland in her days in Rathfarnham I wondered what was the biggest difference she noticed between the Ireland she first visited in the 1920s and the Ireland of the 1990s:

"The noise! We need to find God, and he cannot be found in noise. God is the friend of silence. See how nature grows in silence; see the stars, the moon and sun, how they move in silence. Is not our mission to give God to the poor? Not a dead God, but a living, loving God. We need silence to be able to touch souls. The essential thing is not what we say, but what God says to us and through us.

"The greatest disease in Ireland and in the West today is not TB or HIV, it is being unwanted, unloved and uncared for. We can cure physical diseases with medicine but the only cure for loneliness, despair and hopelessness is love. There are many in the world who are dying for a piece of bread but there are many more dying for a little love. The poverty I see in Ireland today is a different kind of poverty – it is not only a poverty of loneliness but also of spirituality. There's a hunger for love, as there is a hunger for God. As a people and as a society, if we command our wealth we shall be rich and free, if our wealth commands us we shall be poor indeed.

"The type of poverty in Ireland now is all over the western world. I was in London not so long ago and I went to see the homeless people where our Sisters have a soup kitchen. One man, who was living in a cardboard box, held my hand and said: 'It's been a long time since I felt the warmth of a human hand.'

"In New York our Sisters went to a room from which a bad odour was coming. When the room was broken into, they found a woman who had been dead four or five days. No one had come to see her. They did not even know her name. Many of the people are known only by the numbers of their rooms or apartments. One of the greatest diseases is to be nobody to no one.

"Once I took a dying woman from the streets and I told the Sisters that I would take care of her. I did for her all that my love could do. I put her in bed, and there was such a beautiful smile on her face. She took hold of my hand, and she said two words only, 'Thank you' – and she died. I could not help examining my conscience before her, and I asked what would I say if I was in her place. My answer was very simple. I would have tried to draw a little attention to myself. I would have said, 'I am hungry, I am dying, I am cold, I am in pain' or something else, but she gave much, much more. She gave me her grateful love.

"I find the poverty of the West so much more difficult to remove. When I pick up a person from the street, hungry, and I give them a plate of rice, a piece of bread, I have satisfied, I have removed that hunger. But a person that is shut out, that feels unwanted, unloved, terrified, the person that has been thrown out from society – that poverty is so hurtful and so much, that I find it very difficult. Our Sisters are working amongst that kind of people in countries like Ireland.

"In Ireland and in the West at large, there is loneliness which I call the leprosy of the West. In many ways it is worse than our poor in Calcutta. In Calcutta, the poor, they share. I recall a family of six that was starving when our Sisters found them. They gave the women some rice. But first, they divided it into two portions and gave half to another family that was also starving.

"God's own image is in every single child, no matter what that child is, disabled or beautiful or ugly – it's God's beautiful image created for greater things – to love and be loved. That is why you and I and all of us must insist to preserve the gift of God, for it is something very beautiful. That little one who is unwanted, what a terrible suffering that is! Today it is the greatest disease, to be unwanted, unloved, just left alone, a throwaway of society. There are thousands, millions of people who die for lack of bread. There are thousands, millions, of human beings who grow weak for lack of a little love because they would like to be recognised, even if just a little. Jesus becomes weak and dies in them.

"Being unwanted is the most terrible disease that human beings can experience. The only cure can lie in willing hands to serve and hearts to go on loving them. In one of our houses there was a woman who was dying. She felt the presence of God with us and said: 'I've lived like an animal in the street but I will die like an angel.' Those who die with us, die in peace. For me that is the greatest development of the human life, to die in peace and in dignity, for that is for eternity. I come to Ireland as often as I can because I want to share this message with the people."

An Audience with Mother Teresa

Mother Teresa often responded to Ireland's call down the years and came to visit Ireland on numerous occasions. On May 31st 1993, she travelled to Dublin and on June 1st she addressed a big crowd of people at the Marian shrine in Knock.

On a drab and uninspiring evening in August 1879 a small community witnessed the apparition at Knock, through sheets of driving rain and piercing wind. The visitation gave hope to a famine-struck persecuted region. One hundred and fourteen years later Mother Teresa came to visit one of Ireland's most famous places of pilgrimage.

Many pilgrims were armed with flasks, mustard-laden ham sandwiches and raincoats. Some had travelled by train via Claremorris station. The station was done up in blue and white, the traditional colours of the Virgin. The stampede for the bus to Knock was like a scene from the Battle of the Alamo. The first impression was of a row of cars and hedges – the car registrations were of each of the thirty-two counties with plenty of "continental" cars in their midst. The traditional hawkers had been displaced to the more sightly purpose-built side where people could engage in business or drink the soup of secularism depending on one's point of view. Tourists purchased the obligatory holy-water bottle and chatted amiably to the stall owners. Pamphlets and prayer booklets abounded.

Stewards decked out in bright green sashes directed the teeming crowds like traffic police. One man joked that he was seeking a cure for baldness. A distraught lady praying to give up cigarettes was horrified to discover herself trying to light a fag with the same matches she used to light a candle in the grotto.

A woman with a sick baby rushed to greet Mother Teresa. In a plea from the mother's heart, her help was sought. To that mother this visitor from India was both awe-inspiring and an intimate friend.

We all live with deep frustrations and broken dreams. Rather than face the incompleteness of our lives and our feelings of loneliness and inner emptiness, we often desperately search for companionship in order to feel a sense of belonging. At the root of much of our restlessness is an impatient waiting for something to fulfil our lives: a marriage partner, power, fame. We refuse to shed dreams that are manifestly not for us. We stand before life with unrealistic expectations. We all seek intimacy and healing in our lives. We seek intimacy because we cannot live without love and affection. We seek healing because we experience sickness and pain.

The Basilica was full of holy people – so-called "ordinary people" whose generosity towards God was as tangible a sign of divine love as anyone was ever entitled to expect. Down through history many people have been considered good, such as Jesus Christ, St Francis of Assisi and Mother Teresa. What is noteworthy about these people is that, their great moments apart, it is their simplicity which chiefly colours our conception of them. On closer examination we see that their lives were full of weakness. Frailty and holiness went hand in hand on that day in Knock.

Some pilgrims felt that they were on holy ground – each stone, each blade of grass outside, each singing bird flying over the Basilica, each voice, each smiling face, each concerned look, all and each, each and all were holy, radiant ornaments on the sacred altar of creation, jewels in God's sanctuary. They felt comfort in the thought that although all is passing, all is eternal. In the stillness of her soul Mother Teresa sensed the eternal movement; in the tireless running of the energetic children with their thoughts on sugar sticks and chocolate, she saw deeper into the abundant calm.

Some pilgrims seem soaked in a heavy despondency as if some totally melancholy spirit brooded over the place. The oldest pilgrims were devout and sad, wondering would they be alive to make the trip next year. Illness was sucking the vitality out of many as a bee sucks honey out of a flower. The Basilica was a monument to broken hearts and foiled aspirations, to innumerable tales of sadness and dawning shreds of hope.

A person, it is held, can become accustomed to anything, but suffering for many of these people was a recurring nightmare. Often during severe illness it is difficult not to succumb to a great sense of the desolation of life which sweeps all round like a tidal wave, drowning all in its blackness. The real miracle of Knock is that the black clouds are lifted, at least temporarily. The most frequent healing is on the inside.

To look behind the faces of some of the people was

to discover the harshest realities of human existence. They were searching the hidden places of the mind for the elusive memory of overwhelming happiness. Most were there for just a glimpse of Mother Teresa. Wheelchairs were lined up in almost military style and priests in white robes with blue crosses anointed those in them with oil held by volunteers. The patients were clearly heartened by this attention and blessing. Inside the bright, celestial-blue Basilica a wonderful choir sang inspiring messages.

Nowhere were Emily Dickinson's observations more apparent:

> *Hope is the thing with feathers*
> *That perches in the soul,*
> *And sings the tune without the words,*
> *And never stops at all.*

The atmosphere was electric, like a revivalist meeting with a touch of fanaticism. The crowd waited for her to come up to the podium like a presidential candidate. As Mother Teresa spoke all eyes were on her, seemingly transfixed. It appeared that if she had asked them to try walking on water they would have been happy to do so.

Her influence was great because she expressed herself simply and in a way everyone could understand. Her concepts were universal – trust, surrender, love, mercy – but her genius was to revitalise them and give them back their original beauty. Everything about her was full of life and conviction and she impressed her own "stamp" on a fresh and original expression of the Christian message. For many she was an inspiring shortcut to the gospel message.

Her message sometimes echoed St John of Cross: "Where there is no love, put love, and you will find love . . . in the evening of our lives we will be judged on our love."

The gospels are full of Good News – God's love for us, hope, life, wisdom, truth and healing. In Knock on that June day Mother Teresa was the calm at the centre of a storm. She said: "Our Lady loves Ireland. So, let us make a strong resolution that in this beautiful country no child may be unwanted."

She was followed by the Archbishop of Tuam, Dr Joseph Cassidy.

A man approached her with a sick young child cradled in his arms, another witness in the court of human suffering. He was looking for a blessing and hoping that he would get a miracle cure from her healing hands.

Like many in the sunny crowd a woman pushed forward and asked Mother Teresa to take her hands and said: "I am expecting a baby in November so please pray for me." Quick as a flash Mother Teresa responded: "I will pray that she will be a Missionary of Charity."

As a young girl Mother Teresa had a great devotion to the Virgin Mary. As a child in Albania, like most

Irish people at the time, Mother Teresa welcomed the fine weather by joining the rush to erect a May altar in honour of Our Lady, that month being considered the special month of Our Lady. Boxes, tea-chests and all kinds of idle implements were draped with white sheets to make homemade altars in family homes. Flowers were piled into jam jars for decoration. The most colourful ceremony of all was the procession from the chapel down to the village. It seemed to be an injunction for the sacred to leave the church and make its home in the hearts of people.

I asked her if she prayed to Our Lady herself:

"One of my favourite prayers is: 'Mary, Mother of Jesus, give me your heart, so beautiful, so pure, so immaculate, so full of love and humility that I may be able to receive Jesus in the Bread of Life, love Him as you loved Him and serve Him in the poorest of the poor.'

"In 1984, the Holy Father was celebrating Mass outside in Saint Peter's Square, and there was a great crowd. A group of Missionaries of Charity was also there. Suddenly it started to rain. I told the Sisters, 'Let us pray a quick novena of *Memorare* to Our Lady so it stops raining.' While we were praying the second *Memorare*, it started to rain even harder. While we prayed the third, the fourth, the fifth, the sixth, the seventh, and the eighth ones, the umbrellas started to close. By the time we finished the ninth prayer, the only open umbrellas were ours; we had worried so much about praying that we had not paid attention to the weather. It had stopped raining."

A New Vision

Kathy Sinnott describes her life in two phases BJ and AJ: "Before Jamie" and "After Jamie". Jamie was only three months old when he first began to exhibit symptoms of autism. For over twenty-five years Kathy has campaigned to ensure that no more young people will ever have to "share the scrapheap with Jamie" and, like him, arrive at eighteen uneducated. She too was in the congregation on that day in Knock and was profoundly influenced by the experience:

"*'God doesn't require us to be successful. He only asks us to try.'* I was deeply affected when I first came across these words of Mother Teresa. For days after, her sentences replayed continuously in my head and heart. In our culture we are groomed to seek success. In school, we are taught its importance. We study the great achievements and achievers in History class and in our literature the make-believe ones. In Maths, we successfully solve the problem or fail. In school, we are constantly ranked from most successful to least. We carry this bias towards success into our working lives and into our families and relationships. We learn to judge everything that we and others do by the success of the outcome. Mother Teresa's message is absolutely clear. God does not rank us by success. He does not even require it. He just asks us to try. He asks us to be willing even if we are not able. I felt a huge weight was lifted. I wanted to help those who needed help but felt ill equipped. My sense of inadequacy was often paralysing.

"Mother's message that I should try to leave the outcome to God was liberating. I was freed from a need to be skilled, in charge, from having to know everything. I was also freed from discouragement. I could serve, focusing on the effort and the love and concern that I could bring to it rather than the outcome. It was of course not as easy as that. I had to train myself to let go of success. I remember one of the first things I did to detach myself from a reliance on success was to walk into a messy room, tidy it and then walk away without the satisfaction of a last look at the clean room. It may seem a small thing but it was difficult to do as it was liberating. It helped me become less precious about everything I did.

"Being very grateful for this growing freedom, I went to pray with Mother Teresa in Knock in June 1993. Bringing a car full of children on the five-hour journey to Knock is penance for all concerned. But for Jamie, who has profound disabilities and was hypersensitive to sound and touch, being bundled into the car was especially trying. There were crowds at the shrine that day so we staked out a little patch of grass and waited. Martina, a friend, took Jamie into the Basilica where Mother Teresa was going to pray with those who were sick or disabled. Though there were many people waiting to meet Mother Teresa, she found time to hold Jamie's hands and pray with him. The ride home was quiet. Praying with Mother Teresa had left us all prepared to accommodate each other no matter how cramped, cold and hungry we were.

"As I drove home I reflected on the wonderful day. I came knowing that Mother was heroic but I left knowing that she was reachable. Her words were simple, her gentle challenges to us were within everyone's reach. But what about the children's reaction, especially the reaction of the younger children and of Jamie? What were they responding to? I was convinced that it was her love. Her love of God, her love of us. In the Mass, we had each been included in Mother's Eucharistic embrace and for a period of grace we seemed to remain there."

Cry Freedom

On December 9th 1979 Mother Teresa arrived in Oslo to receive the Nobel Prize for Peace. In her life she received many honours in Ireland. In 1995 the Royal College of Surgeons in Dublin awarded her their highest award, an Honorary Fellowship of the College. She joined such illustrious winners as Nelson Mandela and former US President Jimmy Carter.

Two years earlier Mother Teresa had come to Ireland to receive the highest honour the Irish state could confer on her at the invitation of the then Lord Mayor of Dublin, Gay Mitchell TD. To understand Gay Mitchell's family devotion to Mother Teresa it was necessary to journey with him on a tapestry of memories back to his childhood:

"Well, as a young person I was brought up to believe in God and we had the rosary daily without exception. Of course every day for Lent we had Mass in the morning at 7 a.m. and my father would have the breakfast ready for the family when the rest got back. We were also taught to be non-judgemental of others and to respect other people's point of view. So from an early age and to this day God and prayer are important parts of my life. I believe in constant prayer, on the way to work or school. When should we pray? *'In all dangers, temptations and afflictions.'*

"I'm a practising Catholic but I'm also a practising sinner and my mother in particular had the attitude that if you had to repent for your sins, the best way to do it was by going to the church. I go to the church as a means of repentance but more importantly as a way of keeping in touch with God."

Religion was not just for Sundays in the Mitchell household.

"Apart from prayer it was driven into us to be honest. My mother's favourite saying was, *'Honesty is the best policy.'* Another big thing was your word of honour. She would always urge us to keep our word.

"My father died when I was five. Much of what I know of him came from the rest of my family, like my late brother Jim, because my memories of my dad are not very strong. I know from Jim that our father was an extraordinarily charitable man, to a very unwise extent. He gave away lots to charitable cases when we had very little to spare. On one occasion our electricity was cut off for two reasons, in part because he was giving money away to people with problems. For instance, on one occasion he brought home a traveller woman and seven children and my mother who was already stretched to the limit to feed her own family had to try and accommodate them. They were given food that night and a bath and given our beds to sleep in. We had to sleep on the floor. The next day they were sent off with food parcels. Of course my mother afterwards had no idea how she was going to put food on the table for the next week.

"My father used to do the 'Spot the Ball' competition in one of the English newspapers. He won the competition and shortly after he got a cheque for £7, which was a lot of money back then. My father always said he could see the profile of the traveller woman on the cheque. Overwhelmingly, there was a huge message from my parents that you should give.

"This kind of spirit was very prominent in the area I grew up in, in Inchicore. The tone was set by the Oblate Fathers, the Christian Brothers and the Sisters of Mercy in the schools. There were a lot of practical initiatives to help the poor – with the penny dinners and so on. My mother too was very involved in the local church. I was involved in St Vincent de Paul, and actually met my wife through that. I think our family background is one of the main reasons why I have such admiration for Mother Teresa. Her faith is rock solid. She absolutely has no doubts about her beliefs. She never has to question them in any way though she is tolerant of other people's views. It was right that the Irish people should honour her and people like Nelson Mandela by giving them the freedom of Dublin because of the moral inspiration they provide."

Once he became Lord Mayor in 1992 Gay Mitchell knew that one of the privileges of his position was the power to confer the Freedom of the City on the person of his choice.

"It has to be handled very carefully and you need to bring the County Council with you. If you can do that you can do pretty much anything you want. One female councillor was initially opposed. When I floated the idea she said: 'You're not serious. She is opposed to divorce.' I replied: 'Well, what do you expect? She's a Catholic nun.'

"At the time, the Church was under a lot of pressure after the news that the much-admired Bishop Éamon Casey had fathered a child – though nothing like it is now. I felt that a lot of good people in the Church were doing an awful lot of great work but were not getting recognition. When I conferred the Freedom of the City in Dublin on Mother Teresa I pointed out that one of the reasons was to recognise not just her work but the extraordinary commitment of the many dedicated religious. Afterwards somebody told me that I was the only Lord Mayor that was ever mentioned in an Archbishop of Dublin's Lenten Pastoral Letter. Desmond Connell mentioned me because I had singled out the good work done by religious and priests.

"I asked the then PRO of Dublin City Council, the late Noel Carroll, to get me a number for Mother Teresa. He did and asked me if I wanted him to ring her for me. I told him I wanted to do it myself. Within seconds of dialling a voice answered and I said: 'I'm the Lord Mayor of Dublin and I want to speak to Mother Teresa of Calcutta.' The voice answered: 'Speaking.' It surprised me that she was at the end of the line. I told her what I had in mind and we eventually agreed a time for the ceremony. Closer to the time the Provincial of her Sisters in London rang me and said that she also wanted to visit Knock and Belfast. I arranged that she could that."

Given Mother Teresa's lifestyle the ceremony would have to be unlike previous ones:

"When she was coming I decided that we should do things differently for her. We normally have a reception but I decided that it was not appropriate to do it in the normal way. So I decided that we would have a breakfast for the poor of the city – though we phrased it a little differently.

"The ceremony was televised live by RTÉ. After I said my bit, she spoke powerfully without using a single note. She was a very diminutive woman but she had such a strong hold on the crowd. Before the trip she had broken her ribs and was in great pain. After the ceremony was over everybody was trying to touch her and I put my arm around her because I was genuinely fearful for her.

"On the day she arrived I had met her in the airport and we had chatted. When I got home my wife Norma asked me: 'What's Mother Teresa like?'

"I replied: 'Do you know – she's like an old aunt I've known all my life.'

"After the ceremony I brought her back to where she was staying with her Sisters in Donore Avenue. They were trying to set up a youth club. She asked me to help them out with that project and I agreed to do so. Then she said: 'Do you know, Lord Mayor, I feel I've known you all my life.' It was a very strange thing to say.

"All nuns in my view are people with their minds on business. If you went into a hospital years ago that was run by nuns, you knew immediately it was run by nuns because their hospitals were clean and well-ordered. When we spoke about the youth club it was obvious she was very clued in.

"She gave me a Miraculous Medal which I still wear to this day," he displayed the medal to confirm this fact, "and a statue of Our Lady. She also gave some medals to my family. She asked Norma if she would give her our daughter for the Missionaries of Charity.

"I gave her a Waterford Cut Glass Celtic Cross about a foot and a half high. It was one of a kind. When I was finishing my term as Lord Mayor, Waterford Glass told me that they would like to present me with any suite of their glass because I had given them a lot of publicity through presentations and so on. I said I didn't want any glass but what I would like was a replica of the Celtic Cross they made for Mother Teresa. I still have it a home and it is nice to think that it is one of a brace.

"I thought she was extraordinary for her ordinariness. Yet she also seemed very saintly. Although she was very composed, dignified and unassuming she was one of those people you meet that you could never forget. I've never met anyone like her. She was a one-off. She was what you would imagine a saint to be. She wrote me a very nice letter afterwards which I have framed at home in which she thanked me for receiving her."

Senator Feargal Quinn (of Superquinn, one of Ireland's largest supermarket chains) also played his part in Mother Teresa's Freedom of Dublin:

"I have very personal memories of meeting

Mother Teresa. On April 14th 1993, Lord Mayor Gay Mitchell invited me to attend a meeting in the Mansion House as Mother Teresa was coming to Dublin to receive the Freedom of the City. Due to my experience in organising the Christmas Day Dinner in the Mansion House for over thirty years, Mayor Mitchell asked me to organise a breakfast on Wednesday, June 2nd, in the Mansion House for Mother Teresa. He explained that Mother Teresa wanted the breakfast to include the poor of Dublin and the various charitable organisations.

"It totally caught the imagination of Superquinn – everyone wanted to be involved. In fact, so many people volunteered to work at the breakfast that we had to hold a lottery in each shop. The preparations for it created the most amazing atmosphere. We handled every aspect of the occasion from security within the Mansion House, to decorating the Round Room, table setting, as well as cooking and serving up a full Irish breakfast for 500 guests from multi-denominational charities.

"My Executive Assistant, Anne O'Broin, and I had a photograph taken with Mother Teresa. A montage of that and the other photographs of that day still receive pride of place in the canteens of the fourteen Superquinns that existed in 1993.

"It was a stunning occasion – one which everyone involved in will never forget. For such a tiny woman she made a huge impression on each of us."

Men of the Cloth

Mother Teresa also left her mark on a generation of Irish priests. One man largely responsible for this was Monsignor Niall Ahern:

"I was Director of Formation in the seminary in Maynooth for many years in the 1980s and 1990s. One of the projects I arranged was for our seminarians to go to work in their summer holidays in Mother Teresa's hostel for the dying in Calcutta so they could experience Christian love in action in a very meaningful way and see up close and personal what service means. We invited her to come to Maynooth in 1990 to give the annual Trócaire lecture. Mother Teresa held a prayer service in the college chapel and then had a private meeting with seminarians and staff. She presented us each with a gift, a rosary. I got to know her reasonably well and was invited to go to India and other places down the years to give retreats to her Sisters. I also drove her to Áras an Uachtaráin to meet Mary Robinson. They had a private meeting and got on very well."

The respect in which Mother Teresa held Monsignor Ahern was indicated by the fact that he was invited to be one of the concelebrants of the Mass to mark her beatification. Ireland was to reap a handsome dividend from their relationship:

"After I left Maynooth in the early 1990s I went back to my own diocese of Elphin to work as a diocesan administrator in Sligo. I invited Mother Teresa to come down to us and when she came to us she was presented with the Freedom of Sligo. "Subsequently her Sisters came to set up a convent in Sligo in 2000. The new convent was the congregation's gift to mark the Millennium. Originally the Sisters had planned to open the new convent in Darjeeling where in 1946 Mother Teresa had experienced her call to follow Christ into the slums to serve Him among the poorest of the poor. Her Sisters bring a contemplative presence to Sligo."

When in Rome

As so many of her Sisters do their studies and training in Rome, Mother Teresa was a frequent visitor to the Eternal City. There she came into contact with many Irish seminarians and priests who were studying or working there. Many were profoundly influenced by that contact. A case in point was a Franciscan priest from Dublin, Gerald Evans, now based in Costa Rica. His Roman journey came via a circuitous route:

"My family had a long association with the Franciscans. After I left school I worked initially in the travel industry both in Ireland and in London. There I began to rethink my life project and decided to commit myself to a life of working with the poor. After I joined the Franciscans in 1977 and studied in Killarney and Galway, I was sent to Rome for three years in 1981.

"When I was in Ireland I had worked with the Simon Community and had a strong feeling for street people. One evening in Rome I was coming home when I saw Mother Teresa's Sisters attending immigrants on the street. The Franciscans allowed me to work with these Sisters in that way. I met Mother Teresa shortly after that in 1982. What struck me first was her size – she was so tiny. I had the same sense meeting her as I did when I met Pope John Paul II – that I was in the presence of someone who lived a totally integrated life, a life of faith.

"It was very obvious to me that Mother Teresa was so much more than the Mother Teresa I knew from the television. She allowed God to work in her and everything she did pointed to God. She felt that she was not important but she was trying to provide people with a window into God. She did not allow any obstacles like her own ego to come into the way of her union with God.

"She was operating on another level. I know that in recent years there has been a lot of emphasis on structural change. Mother Teresa's focus was on interior change. She believed the way to change the world was to change people's hearts. If the heart was changed the world could be changed – but only God could change people's hearts. She always stressed that the only difference between us and the poor was that we had walls and cars. She spoke once in Harvard University and said that poverty and misery were not just on the street but in everybody's homes. The poor mirror our own vulnerability so what everybody needs is a mutual healing process. One of her great achievements was to bring together people who would never meet normally. Directly and indirectly she connected and continues to connect so many people across the globe. In this way she has helped so many people to find the hidden hand of God. She believed in the divine presence and privilege of the poor and this was why what was most needed was a whole process of conversion of people, an interior purification or as she would have put it a 'purity of heart'.

"You really felt that when she was looking at you she was looking through you or into you. I remember when I spoke to her I told her that I was studying theology and asked her if she had any advice for me. She immediately directed me to go to the Eucharist and the poor. She was an intensely practical person – not a theologian nor someone who was bogged down by theory. She was directing me to make the most of my life by finding God in the privileged places by meeting the poor and following Jesus. I met her four times and each time I felt that she had one foot in the Blessed Sacrament Chapel and the other foot on the streets with the poor. Although the meetings I had with her were short they had the most profound impact on me because you only needed a short time with Mother Teresa to realise that the secret of life was being revealed. She did not preach it but she lived it with a passion."

Like so many Irish priests before and since Gerald continues to take inspiration in his priestly duties from the life of Mother Teresa:

"No doubt my subsequent life has been heavily influenced by my meetings with Mother Teresa. After my time in Rome I worked for a number of years in El Salvador which was in the midst of a civil war at the time. I then moved to my current base in Costa Rica. I was immediately struck by the fact that there were so many people on the streets in Costa Rica. I began a new project called Franciscan Dawn where we go out among the poor every Sunday, inspired directly by Mother Teresa's work. I also work in a shelter for homeless people with a young lay woman called Kattia who takes the same approach to the poor that Mother Teresa pioneered. In some respects she reminds me of Mother Teresa because of her commitment and her contentment. So while Mother Teresa died thirteen years ago she still lives on and I try in my own way to work in her spirit."

From Cavan to Here

Even the Irish priests in Rome who never met Mother Teresa were impressed by her. Among their number is Cavan native and former head of the Redemptorist Order in Ireland, Raphael Gallagher.

"Inflation is always dangerous. It devalues. This is true about economics. But it is also true about religion. There were so many people declared as Blessed or Saint by Pope John Paul II that I, for one, had difficulty keeping up with the names. Part of me was saying, 'You can never have too many models for the Christian life', but there was another part whispering 'What is the point of all this blessed-making and saint-making, and is it devaluing the whole exercise?'

"With Mother Teresa I didn't have this doubt. Partly because I had decided that she was an extraordinary example of dedication to the poor well before Rome made any official pronouncement about it. That rang true to a deep conviction of mine. Let the people decide who the holy ones are, and if Rome wants to confirm this, let them.

"The impression she left on me is explained by a simple fact. I still call her Mother Teresa, even though her official Roman title is Blessed Teresa of Calcutta. It is the same thing with Padre Pio in my case. I never refer to his now proper Roman title (Saint Pio of Pietracina) because I am not sure people would know who I was talking about.

"To have a Mother as a model, and a Father as a model in another way, that is no bad thing and it explains part of my fascination with Mother Teresa, as it does with Padre Pio.

"Teresa left the impression on me as the mother who looks out for the weaker members of the family.

I remember a TV interview with her, in one of the orphanages she founded. The presenter said, 'What a wonderful honour it is for me to meet you, Mother.' To which he got the sharp answer: 'There is no honour in that. You are honoured to be meeting these poor orphans whom nobody wants.'

"I never met her, but she was so often on TV I felt I knew her. Would I have liked her as a person? Curiously, I think not. The smile covered a tough side to her character. But I still admire her, and her memory inspires me. As a mother who is concerned for the members of the family who have the toughest times.

"She got a lot of public recognition, so she hardly needs my little words of praise. But two of the biggest honours she got confirm my impression of a caring mother. She was the very first person to be nominated for the John 23rd Peace Prize in 1971, and of course she got the Nobel Prize for Peace. That is what her memory means for me, too. There is no possibility of peace in society if justice is not done to the oppressed person. There are many ways of working for justice, and Mother Teresa's is one of them. I do not dwell much on her personality or her fame, or even the fact that Rome has declared her Blessed. I remember a mother who worked for justice, in her way, and so remains a beacon that helps me to encourage all those who work for justice, in very different ways. What they are doing is noble, because they are working for peace, as Mother Teresa did."

Children of a Lesser God?

Although a number of the Irish seminarians who met Mother Teresa in Rome are no longer in the priesthood, they continue to be heavily influenced by her inspiration. One such former seminarian is Dubliner Paul Kelly who has got involved in the fight against child labour in Guatemala:

"The existence of child labour poses a serious challenge for the Christian community. Our search for the face of Christ cannot be authentic until we honestly confront the social structures that cause parents to feel that there is no option for them but to reluctantly send their children into bonded labour.

"Other people said great things about poverty. To take one example President Dwight D Eisenhower once said: 'Every gun that is made, every warship launched, every rocket fired, signifies a theft from those who hunger and are not fed, those who are cold and have not clothes. The world in arms is not spending money alone. It's spending the sweat of its labourers, the genius of its scientists and the hopes of its children.' Mother Teresa never said fine words like that but she did not need to because she spoke louder and more effectively by her actions.

"Since I met Mother Teresa I always had a desire to do some work in the Third World because of the passion she spoke about the poor. I just always believed we had everything easy over here and we had a huge debt to pay to people less fortunate than us.

"On my kitchen wall I have the words of Audrey Hepburn: 'For a slim figure, share your food with the hungry. For lovely eyes, seek out the good in people. For an attractive face, speak words of kindness. For poise, walk with the knowledge that you will never walk alone.' Like the Beatitudes those are easy words to say but much harder to live by. Every time I read them I can see Mother Teresa in my head because she was the only person I have met who fully lived up these lofty sentiments. She lived by the ideal that kindness is difficult to give away, because it keeps coming back."

From the moment he entered the troubled country Paul was confronted by intense need. To see this on television is akin to watching *Desperate Housewives* or *The Simpsons*.

"You say to yourself this cannot really happen. But when the stark reality is but feet away from you, it is frightening in the extreme."

The whole area was locked into the monstrous barbarism of child labour:

"You could not but be moved by what you saw. I think of getting on a bus to go to work and there would be kids as young as nine and ten there with little machetes going off to cut down trees to make a living. Child labour is horrific to see."

Exposure to this environment was to be a watershed for Paul Kelly. Like Mother Teresa before him, he was not content to curse the darkness – he wanted to light a candle. He knew that charity was not enough. His is a philosophy of a hand-up not a hand-out. The key was sustainable development. Accordingly, he set up a shoe-making business, drawing on the work of a group of women in Guatemala who had formed a co-op. Every day though he thinks back to his days in Rome:

"St Francis of Assisi famously said it is in giving that we receive. Mother Teresa did more than alert and alarm anyone willing to listen. Her work strikingly dramatised the poverty of the modern world, perilously ruled by self-interest and economic power. Her enduring power is in her capacity to stir our resolve and strengthen the collective will to change. She never doubted that a small group of committed people with ideas and vision can change the world. Why? It is the only thing that ever has. She embodied what is best in us all because she lived by the motto that giving in its purest form expects nothing in return. I have never forgotten her. She changed my life and I feel her presence every day."

Voluntary Effort

One of the consequences of Mother Teresa's many visits to Ireland was that many Irishwomen were inspired to join her in her work. In the early years that was always to follow her into the Missionaries of Charity but increasingly, in more recent years, the women who have followed her to India have gone as volunteers.

In 1991 at the age of twenty-four a nurse from Galway, Ann-Marie Burke, took a career break to work as a volunteer with Mother Teresa:

"I really wanted to go to work with Mother Teresa since I was a teenager because I thought she was amazing, but I did not feel the life of a nun was for me so I made the decision to write to her and offer my services to her. She invited me to go to India and share her work for the poor of Calcutta.

"As Christians we are challenged by Jesus to work alongside the poor and to empower them to live with dignity, satisfying their need for food, health care, clothing, housing and education. The poor need help today not next week.

"We are all children of God. We need to try to make sure that those with nothing get something. That's why I wanted to go. I wouldn't say that I was exceptionally religious but I had always tried to live my life on the basis of the words from the Bible: *'Do unto others as you would like to be done unto you.'*

"There have been so many times when we faced insurmountable obstacles and all of a sudden, almost as if by a small miracle, the problem vanished. This kind of thing has happened too often to be simply a coincidence. Not a day goes by without something extraordinary happening."

Angela's thinking changed because of the work experiences with Mother Teresa.

"There is a need for a new approach which takes

account of the need to build new relationships of justice between the haves and the have-nots. Justice is like motherhood, Christmas Day and apple pie. Nobody could object to it. The problem is that everybody is for it in principle but for how many does it translate into practical action? The litmus test for our Christianity will not be the number of nice phrases we trot out but how we live. This is a challenge that we must confront individually and collectively.

"Above all I have learned from Mother Teresa to wonder at the simplicity of life; through her I have developed a profound respect for the poor. I discovered what it means to work in faith and am much more tolerant of other people and other cultures. My experiences in India have caused me to become more aware of the injustices in Ireland. I am troubled by the fact that despite the great economic success we enjoyed, the gulf between rich and poor continues to widen.

"I think it was such a privilege to work with Mother Teresa and just to meet and know her. The poor and sick people I worked with became wise teachers in many ways. They provide the answers and the questions of how we could all appreciate each day as a gift from God. They taught me about the heart-wrenching sorrow and grief that the families go through because of poverty. They have given me new horizons of hope in my life. The greatest gift anyone could give these people is the gift of their time. We know there are many calls on people's generosity. But a little goes a long way in a country as poor as India. These people are our neighbours. The homeless children have no families, no love, no voice and no rights. They need someone to speak up for them, they need people to look out for them rather than look away, they need our concern. We need to work hard to give them back their childhood and give them something to look forward to – a decent life.

"Each day spent with Mother Teresa was like a life of a rainbow of miracles. I was so blessed to be doing that work in her company."

Summer Holiday

Every year thousands of Irish students seek the sun spots of Europe for what is known as "the Leaving Cert. holiday". An increasing number of students though are finding alternative ways of spending the summer months in a way that allows them to help others. A case in point is a young student from Trinity College, Katy Dobey, who gave up her entire summer holidays to work with an organisation called Prayas (a Hindi word meaning endeavour) in Kolkata (what we call Calcutta), which is one of India's largest non-profit organisations. Based in Delhi, it strives to protect the rights of those on the margins of Indian society and helps thousands of people in seven states across India. Katy wanted to walk metaphorically in the footsteps of Mother Teresa and to work with poor children in India.

"My job was to teach English in the school that Prayas runs. I counted thirty-six children in the room and they could be very restless at times – so it was hard work! My primary objective was to give the children a sense that they are worthwhile; cared for and most importantly that they are loved."

In July 2009 Katy got the opportunity to literally walk in the footsteps of Mother Teresa:

"Smothering heat enveloped us as we stepped out of the airport and into Kolkata. There were five of us taking this weekend trip. We made up almost half of a team of Suas Volunteers, based in Delhi, teaching in Alternative Education Centres. These Centres are run by an NGO called Prayas, which focuses on eradicating child labour. So, the summer was full of contradictions. We were guided to a taxi by a self-assured, street-wise, little boy of about ten, who pimped taxis to tourists. Here we were, actively working to prevent child labour, yet being guided by a child worker from airport to taxi. India is like that. Things happen quickly. Your conscience is always questioned and questioning.

"Kolkata was of interest to me from the start. It's the most obvious place for any Irish person to visit in India. Everyone's heard of Mother Teresa and volunteers are doing Trojan work in this most densely populated city in the world. Because of the connection with

Mother Teresa, the city had a particular link with Christianity in my mind.

"After searching the guidebook's map for a church, Cuisle, a fellow volunteer, and I set off on our way to St Saviour's Church to feel that in some way we were connected to the Christian links of the city. The service was over. But a young man came over to welcome us and a few minutes later he and the preacher had us in the sacristy eating a packed lunch from the guidebook's recommended 'Kathleen Confectioners'. We happened to have arrived at his Anglican Church on the 600th anniversary of the building's construction and the community was celebrating.

"The young man was training to become a preacher and was very interested in our reasons for visiting. We told him that Kolkata had a particular resonance in Ireland because of its connection with Mother Teresa and Irish missionaries. He knew all about this and I think I saw a certain pride in the connection between his city, religion and charity.

"He was very keen to show us around the city and kept referring to the science museum. For us, being in Kolkata had nothing to do with a science museum. We'd planned to go to Mass and then visit the Mother House. But we didn't want to be rude. We managed to find a compromise. The preacher often visited a Salvation Army orphanage, which he was keen to show us. After that, he would come with us to Mother House, somewhere he'd never been before.

"The three of us hopped on a tram to the orphanage. It was a sad but beautiful place. After two months working with children, trying to improve their education, we really appreciated the difficulty of raising so many children with the care and attention they deserve. Their personal gifts and talents really seemed to have been nurtured. With the language barrier, it's hard to know much about anything, but we felt the warmth and affection in the room. We sat through several cute renditions of Christian songs, complete with actions – even though we'd been told that most of the children were Hindus.

"Taking a rickshaw to Mother House, I was quite excited. It was almost like a rite of passage. Volunteering in India and Mother Teresa go hand in hand. Stepping in the door, we were greeted by two nuns – one handed us a Miraculous Medal, the other gave us a pamphlet. They were very friendly and unquestioningly issued me with a second medal, when I asked for one for my granny.

"Stepping into the white chapel, where Mother Teresa is buried, we were greeted with a passage of petals and Mass said in Chinese. Language didn't matter. We'd arrived. This is what it was all about."

Into the West

Mother Teresa even managed to impinge on one of Ireland's most famous sporting and social occasions –

the Galway Races. The Festival is an adult version of Disneyland. Normal living is magically suspended for a state of communal bliss. It is a licence to thrill and be thrilled. In this corner of the West, punters experience more ups and downs than the Emperor Charlemagne. It is not so much for whom the bell tolls as for whom the wheel of fortune turns. At Galway the devil makes work for idle hands! Even the wisdom of Solomon and the wealth of Croesus would be insufficient to combat the Galway temptations.

In Galway, there are two elements that are never lacking: hope and an incomplete recollection of the past. Different countries have different national characteristics. In France, they are passionate about ideas. If you shoot a man for disagreeing with you about the intricacies of philosophy, then that is a tremendous compliment to the life of the mind. The French, though, do not share the Irish passion for horses. When the Pope visited Ireland in 1979 he celebrated Mass on the racecourse in Galway.

Horses are to Galway what films are to Hollywood; an obsession that sets a pecking order, discussed endlessly and by everyone, complete with its own arcane laws and rituals. The churches of this strange sporting religion are anywhere two or more racing fans are gathered and its gurus are anyone who can hold an audience. Strong men came dangerously close to blubbering. A few get so emotional that they do the unthinkable: they hug without embarrassment. Galway is the best of times.

The late Fr Seán Breen was known as "The Racing Priest". Fr Brian D'Arcy is the unofficial chaplain to the show-business fellowship. Fr Seán had a similar stature in the horseracing community. He had long been recognised as an authority of the turf.

"It's very hard to say how my interest in horses began. My brother Oliver, who's deceased, was a dentist and he was always interested in horses. I acquired my interest in horses from him. Then he went to England. When I was a student in Maynooth and Clonliffe he used to come back and tell me all about Goodwood, Sandown and Cheltenham and I think it got to me. Oliver knew a lot of people in Irish racing, then I developed an interest myself."

Fr Seán took to this new passion with the intensity of a new lover, drinking in every word and gesture. When it came to horses he became as curious as Galileo gazing at the moon through his telescope. His infatuation never wore away. Frocked in full clerical attire with a pair of binoculars draped around his neck, Fr Seán became an integral part of Irish racing culture.

People take their cultural co-ordinates from different sources. A man of sharp intelligence and uproarious humour, Seán Breen took his largely from the racing world. That explains why every other priest in the country counts Pentecost Sunday in terms of Sundays after Easter but Fr Seán counted it in terms of Easter and the Punchestown Festival!

"John Maloney, the manager of Galway races, said he was thinking of having Mass said on the Sunday at the race-track an hour or two before the meeting began, weather permitting, and invited me to do so. We had a lovely venue in the amphitheatre and a lovely atmosphere with a choir. About 400 people attended made up of trainers, jockeys, owners and public. I have been saying Mass there since then. I think the only other person who said Mass on Galway Racecourse was the Pope!"

Fr Seán was also a big admirer of Mother Teresa and based a homily at one of his Masses on the Galway Racecourse about her.

"I knew that when I mentioned her in Galway I would get a receptive audience because Irish people had such respect for Mother Teresa. The dark night is experienced today in the emotional impoverishment in which many people live. Her legacy can be seen in the number of Sisters and associated lay people who take inspiration from her life. However, the task of interpreting her vision for today and tomorrow is proving a difficult one for us. She offered a new model of leadership which is more circle than pyramid – which is more at the heart, rather than from the top. Her motto could have been: "I am, because we are; we are therefore I am." Mother Teresa challenges Christians in many ways: they must find themselves supporting the widow and the orphan, the cause of the old age pensioner, the homeless, the poor and the outcast. As a result we will question as to why some have an unacceptable standard of living and will want to improve the quality of life for all those we can serve.

"Some years ago a story in the newspapers appeared about a wayward minister of the Anglican Church. The then Archbishop of Canterbury, Dr Runcie, was asked to comment on the incident. He simply said: 'In this earthly tabernacle there are many mansions and they are all made of glass.' Dr Runcie was highlighting the importance of compassion and sensitivity in human relationships. In the way she reached out to others Mother Teresa gave an inkling to the meaning of the saying 'actions speak louder than words'. She lived what Thomas Merton wrote: *'With those for whom there is no room is Jesus.'*

"In her ministry she was inspired by the parable of the Good Samaritan with the poor seen as a vessel for unconditional love and care, rather than prejudice or punishment. We used to walk before the poor. Now thanks to her we walk beside them in order to walk behind them."

Chapter 4

Our Friends in the North

The enduring memory of meeting Mother Teresa for the first time is of an incredibly energetic woman, with a radiant smile and a warm voice, who was totally fulfilled in all aspects of her life. Listening to her talking, it was difficult to see her making any concession to despair even when pain was the background music to her life so long or doubting the power of God in her life. Her faith was clearly not simply a consolation or an optional extra as it animated her every waking moment. Sometimes her faith appeared almost child-like. It is the rock-solid, devout faith which has been such a feature of Irish Catholicism. Her certainty could only be envied.

A huge pile of letters lay on the table beside her. Another bundle to add to the thousands of letters from people who have been touched by a simple, yet extraordinary, woman. It was fan mail of pop-star proportions. The irony of all of this is that one suspects that Mother Teresa was a most unlikely and unwilling candidate for celebrity status on a grand scale; not the kind of woman to have her head easily turned by adulation.

Observe the Sons and Daughters of Ulster

Although the newspapers in the late 1960s were full of Vietnam, Martin Luther King and the civil rights struggle in America, the civil war in Biafra, the ferment in the Middle East after the Lightning War the previous June between Israel and her three Arab neighbours Egypt, Jordan and Syria, Mother Teresa was keenly aware of the escalating sectarian tension which preceded the civil rights demonstrations in Northern Ireland.

There has been one controversial chapter in Mother Teresa's association with Ireland. She put her money, or more precisely her Sisters, where her mouth was.

Mother Teresa firmly believed that the moral challenge was not to passively witness history but to transform it. *"What we hope for is what he promised: a new heaven and a new earth."* (2 Pt 3:13) It is hope that sustains us. St Augustine wrote, *"Hope has two lovely daughters: anger and courage."* The anger comes when we share in the hurt of others. We need courage if we are to take the practical steps necessary to transform the situation.

When the Troubles were at their height in 1971 Mother Teresa sent a group of Sisters armed just with bedrolls and a violin to Belfast. They were given a tiny house whose former occupant, a priest, had been murdered. They stated their rationale for coming as: "We have come from Calcutta to try to improve relations between the people in the whole of Belfast in whatever little way we can."

Mother Teresa, though, was keen to play down her involvement in the decision: "I am not the centrepiece. It is Christ using me as His instrument to unite up all the people. This is what I see happening: people coming to meet each other because of their need for God. I felt that if our Sisters could bring people together to talk about God that this would be really wonderful. I hoped it would bring a new glimmer of hope for the community."

According to reports Mother Teresa herself once spent an hour on the phone with Ian Paisley trying to broker a peace deal but it failed.

After only eighteen months, though, her Sisters suddenly withdrew from the province in mysterious circumstances. Speculation was rife that they did so at the request of either the local church authorities or a specific figure within the Church itself.

When I asked her about it Mother Teresa refused to discuss it and merely stated that it was important to always follow God's will even when we did not understand it. When I tried to probe further and asked if there had been resentment that missionary Sisters should come from India to Ireland she merely said: "We are brothers and sisters in the same family, created by the same loving God."

A famous story is told about St Francis of Assisi. One day two young men came to Francis, saying that they wanted to join his friars. Francis looked at them and said, "Before accepting you, I would like you to do something for me." As he said this, he stooped down, picked up two cabbage plants and handed one to each of the two men. Pointing to a small patch of newly dug soil, he asked them to plant the cabbages. They were about to do this, when Francis added, "There is just one more thing. I want you to plant them upside down, with the leaves buried and the roots in the air." Immediately one of the men picked up a trowel, and did what Francis directed. The other politely pointed out that if the cabbages were planted like that they would never grow. This prospective monk was asked to return home while the first man was enthusiastically welcomed into the brotherhood. This type of blind obedience to Church authority was perfectly understandable to Mother Teresa.

I Have a Dream

In an interview Mother Teresa was once asked if the taking of life was ever justified – in war, for example. She replied simply by shaking her head. The interviewer probed further and reminded her that the Church teaches us that there can be a just war.

Mother Teresa continued to shake her head and said: "I can't understand it."

The journalist was still not placated and said: "Catholics have to believe that teaching."

Mother Teresa instantly replied: "Then I am not a Catholic."

I reminded her that in 1981, after she returned from a mission to Ethiopia when a terrible drought threatened thousands of lives, she had written to President Ronald Regan. The American president telephoned her on behalf of the American people and promised her that he would rush in the food and medicine she requested. Did she ever think about using that kind of power in Northern Ireland?

"I wish I had power. Then I would bring peace to Ireland and the world. I want nothing from governments. I simply offer my Sisters to work among the poor and suffering people. We try to bring love and compassion for the unwanted and the unloved. The work of our Sisters reveals to the suffering poor the love of God for them.

"I won't mix in politics. War is the fruit of politics, and so I don't involve myself, that's all. If I get stuck in politics, I will stop loving. Because I will have to stand by one not by all. This is the difference."

In Mother Teresa's perspective the crisis of the age in Northern Ireland was essentially a spiritual crisis, a crisis of our collective souls. The fate of the soul is the fate of the society; the soul is the core, the heart, the inner reality of what makes us human. The conflicts in our society are but symptoms of an inner torment, of our aberrations on our spiritual journey. If we are to restore our society, we must begin in the inside. We all share the guilt for the sins of the past; if we are to be redeemed either on an individual or societal basis, we must be cleansed at a level beyond the scope of sight and sound. Accordingly, she advocated a spiritual solution:

"Holiness is not the luxury of a few. It is everyone's duty: yours and mine. Our works of love are nothing but works of peace. Let us do them with greater love and efficiency. Let us radiate the peace of God and so extinguish the darkness in the world, and in the hearts of all people all hatred and love for power. If you really love that person then it will be easier for you to accept that person and it will be with love and kindness. For that is an opportunity for you to put your love for God in living action.

"A beautiful thing happened in Calcutta. Two young people came to see me, Hindu people. They gave me a very big amount of money. 'How did you get so much money?' I asked them. They answered me, 'We got married two days ago. Before our marriage, we decided we would not have a big wedding feast and we would not buy wedding clothes. We decided that we would give the money we saved to you to feed the people.'

In a rich Hindu family, it is a scandal not to have special wedding clothes and not to have a wedding feast. 'Why did you do that?' I asked them. They answered me, 'Mother, we love each other so much that we wanted to obtain a special blessing from God by making a sacrifice. We wanted to give each other this special gift.' Is that not beautiful? Things like that are happening every day, really beautiful things. We must pull them out. We have to pull out the wonderful things that are happening in Northern Ireland as well as the bad things.

"A Hindu man was once asked: 'What is a Christian?' He responded, 'The Christian is someone who gives.' Give until it hurts, until you feel the pain. Open your hearts to the love God instils in them. God loves you tenderly. What he gives you is not to be kept under lock and key, but to be shared. The more you have, the less you will be able to give. The less you have, the more you will know how to share. Let us ask God, when it comes time to ask him for something, to help us to be generous.

"When I visited China in 1969, one of the Communist Party asked me: 'Mother Teresa, what is a communist to you?' I answered, 'A child of God, a brother, a sister of mine.' 'Well, you think highly of us. But where did you get that idea?' I told him, 'From God himself. He said, "*Truly I tell you, just as you did it to one of the least of these who are members of my family, you did it to me.*"

"In his passion, Jesus taught us to forgive out of love, how to forget out of humility. So let us examine our hearts and see if there is any unforgiven hurt – any unforgotten bitterness. The Spirit pours love, peace, joy into our hearts. We must respond by emptying ourselves of self-indulgence, vanity, anger, and ambition, and by our willingness to shoulder the cross of Christ.

"Let us not use bombs and guns to overcome the world. Let us use love and compassion. Let us preach the peace of Christ as He did. He went about doing good. If everyone could see the image of God in his neighbour, do you think we would need tanks and generals?

"In order to be Christians, we should resemble Christ, of this I am firmly convinced. Gandhi once said that if Christians lived according to their faith, there would be no more Hindus left in India. People expect us to be consistent with our Christian life but in so many areas we are not and that is why we have conflict.

"We all need to be generous. Once we had a great shortage of sugar in Calcutta. One day, a boy about four years old came to see me with his parents. They brought me a small container of sugar. When they handed it to me, the little one told me: 'I have spent three days without eating any sugar. Take it. This is for your children.' Although he could hardly say my name the little one loved with an intense love. We all need to learn from him. Peace and war begin at home. If we truly want peace in Northern Ireland and the world, let us begin by loving one another in our own families. If we want to spread joy, we need for every family to have joy. God has created us so we do small things with great love. I believe that great love, that comes, or should come from our heart, should start at home: with my family, my neighbours across the street, those right next door. And this love should then reach everyone."

Central to this peace process for Mother Teresa was prayer. In Tennyson's incisive observation, *"More things are wrought by prayer than this world dreams of."* She recalled how Pope John Paul II understood this when, on October 27th 1986, he brought leaders of the great religions to pray for peace at Assisi. Before issuing the invitation he had sought the views of the Dalai Lama, the Chief Rabbi of Rome, and the Archbishop of Canterbury, who was secretary general of the World Council of Churches. Fittingly the patron was to be Francis of Assisi, the man whose love for friends, enemies and all creatures meek and tall, has enchanted people of goodwill in all times and places. Representatives of all the religions, the Dalai Lama and Mother Teresa humbly entered the Basilica to be welcomed by the Pope. They came in order for the religions to pray together for world peace, for international justice and for the preservation of our wonderful world. They sang Psalm 148 in Greek: *"Let everything that lives praise the Lord."* Then they journeyed to twelve different places in Assisi where they prayed separately in line with their own traditions, closely united with innumerable people throughout the world, all praying for peace. It is doubtful if there has ever been a greater celebration of unity in diversity and diversity in unity.

The journey to peace would require courage but Mother Teresa felt it was a time for bravery. Saint Francis knew what it was like to go outside his comfort zone. As a young man, often he would ride his horse in the plain below Assisi, where there was a leper colony. It was on one of these occasions that he met a leper face to face. Although terrified of the poor man, Francis dismounted from his horse and ran towards him, offering him money and the kiss of peace. He would cherish this encounter all his life and brought it to his memory before his death. Francis is a prophetic presence who challenges us to change our world today and for each of us to be "the herald of the great king".

Mother Teresa believed that to take us further down the road to atonement we should make the prayer of Saint Francis our own – his prayer before the crucifix which spoke to him and is now venerated in the Basilica of St Clare in Assisi:

Most high, glorious God,
Cast your light into the darkness of my heart.
Give me, Lord, right faith,
Firm hope,

Perfect charity
And profound humility,
With wisdom and perception,
So that I may carry out
What is truly Your holy will.
Amen.

Sorry Seems to be the Hardest Word

Apart from prayer the other essential prerequisite for peace according to Mother Teresa was forgiveness. She believed that essential to the meaning of forgiveness is letting go and that we could not continue to go down the road we spent so many years on of hating those who hurt us – especially as almost with his dying breath Jesus uttered words of forgiveness, in the process elevating forgiveness to the centre of Christianity. Forgiveness operates not just at the personal level but also at the structural level and the institutional level – those in power frequently have necessity to seek forgiveness from the powerless.

She believed that the defeatism we have often witnessed in the dark days of the Troubles was no longer an option. In this perspective the Church does not in any way diminish its vocation to confess and preach Christ when it recognises that the mystery of His salvation offers an embrace of healing mercy in which everyone has a place. The tyranny of the past can be broken; the sin of the past can be healed in the future – not by minimising the seriousness of the past, but by putting the past in the perspective of a different future:

"I once picked up a woman from a garbage dump and she was burning with fever. She was in her last days and her only lament was: 'My son did this to me.' I begged her to forgive her son. I told her that in a moment of madness when he was not himself, he did something he would regret. I asked her to be a mother to him and forgive him. It took me a long time to make her say: 'I forgive my son.' Just before she died, she was able to say that with real forgiveness.

"A young man was dying in one of our homes, but for three or four days fought to prolong his life. The Sister there asked him: 'Why do you continue this fight?' He answered: 'I cannot die without asking forgiveness from my father.' When his father arrived, the youth embraced him and asked forgiveness. Two hours later, the young man passed away peacefully.

"I never forget what happened to our Sisters in Rome, where we work with the volunteers who work with the dispossessed. They go to the poor people's houses. We clean the house and give them a bath, wash their clothes in the house and so on. The Sisters found someone left in a terrible condition. They cleaned his room and washed his clothes and gave him a good bath, but he never spoke.

After two days he told the Sisters, 'You have brought God into my life, bring Father also.'

They went to the parish priest and brought the priest. That man who never spoke, only that sentence he said, made his confession. He made his confession after sixty years, and next morning he died. He died at peace.

"There are so many religions and each one has its different ways of following God. I follow Christ: Jesus is my God. There is only one God and He is God to all; therefore it is important that everyone is seen as equal before God. I've always said we should help a Hindu become a better Hindu, a Muslim become a better Muslim, a Catholic become a better Catholic."

Mother Teresa chose to call a form of newsletter she wrote for her Sisters *Ek Dil*, a Hindi term, an expression describing the unity among the Sisters in their houses all over the globe. *Ek Dil* means "one heart".

"Look what God is doing with nothing. People must believe that it is all His, all His. We must allow God to use us, without adding or subtracting anything."

The Pipes of Peace
On July 8th 1981 Mother visited Corrymeela to talk about peace in a province stained by bloodshed. For all the pain and darkness of the years of the Troubles Mother Teresa knew deep down that the people of Northern Ireland were children of God's light and

delight. When the time was right they too would have the glory of the resurrection when the Risen Son would restore peace. The sorrowful mysteries would become joyful and glorious.

It was exhilarating in the audience to feel this inner peace that her heart had hungered for, a hunger that could only be satisfied with a loving God. She cherished the thought, but such a state of bliss could not be found in this time. A tidal wave of happiness swept over her as she thought of God in heaven. But her joy was short-lived. She saw the families who had lost loved ones before her again. She thought of their bonds of love, with her constant wonder at the mystery of their unending goodness and their need for a new beginning. She had often heard people saying "hope springs eternal", but there were times in the darkest days of the Troubles when hope seemed a nonsense.

Mother Teresa prayed: "Oh my God, help us, give peace to my children. My God, help us." It was a cry of the heart – a prayer born not out of selfishness but out of love and faith.

As Mother Teresa talked, sweet memories were recalled with affection. All the "might-have-beens" were discarded wistfully. The moments of tragedy and heartbreak were momentarily brushed to one side. She wanted to bring peace with an intensity that was almost frightening. Like seeds dreaming of spring beneath the snow, her heart dreamt that she would get to see the Promised Land of Peace within a few more years but the demeanour of the political situation suggested that this was futile. The shadow of death lurked ominously over it like a vulture hovering over its prey. She forced herself to think positively. Her rosary was soothing, almost hypnotic.

On the visit to Northern Ireland the rosary beads Mother Teresa owned never left her. It would have been easy to talk about the political turmoil of the time as a modern-day tragedy. Much too easy. Rather than fall victim to the futility of the "what-might-have-been" and merely offer sympathy or, worse, pity, Mother Teresa wanted to respond to the prayer of Saint Francis and become a channel of peace Rather than brood on the past her concern was to make up for lost time. Each new day was an opportunity to redress the balance and restore the correct relationship between two parts of the Christian family.

Mother Teresa unmasked fear and proclaimed the triumph of love and the victory of a healing God. In her strength and simplicity she touched the core of the human spirit, a woman who found strength in weakness and victory in defeat. Her power was not in what she preached but in what she had come through and lived. Her captivity to the service of the poor helped her to find the secret of transforming her life with meaning and in doing so she became a source of light and life for others as well.

She said on that day that she was beginning to understand more what Jesus dreamed that the kingdom of God really was. Sometime on the days when there were bombings and killings the dream seemed very far away but the thought of the dream should keep us warm. In this kingdom all that has divided people will merge, compassion will be wedded to power, softness will come to a world that is harsh and unkind, all will share equally in the earth's abundance, all will care for the sick and the weak and the old, all will nourish the young and all will cherish life's creatures.

At the end of her talk a well-wisher presented her with the words of the Celtic Blessing:

Deep peace of the running waves to you,
Deep peace of the shining stars to you
Deep peace of the Prince of Peace to you.

In the crowd at the time was Nobel Peace Prize winner Mairéad Corrigan. Ms Corrigan had co-founded the Peace People with Betty Williams in 1976 after three of her sister's children were killed in an accident related to the ongoing violence. Her sister was so overcome by grief that she took her own life.

Asked about her impressions, Ms Corrigan replied:

"Mother Teresa said nothing I had not heard before or read from the gospels, but she brings the whole thing to life. In a gentle but at the same time extraordinarily demanding way, she challenges me to live out personally the Christian life. I think what makes Mother Teresa's words so effective is that she is living out her words in her life. When she tells you that she loves people and is loved by God, one cannot for a moment doubt that fact. Standing on the hill outside the tent (as it was packed) with the gentle rain refreshing me, looking out over the sea, and listening to Mother Teresa saying, 'God loves you,' I felt a deep peace and, though tired, felt the desire to rededicate myself and redouble my efforts for peace."

Ciaran McKeown wrote the Declaration of the Peace People. He too made the trip to Corrymeela. He went on record to state that he went as a gesture of thanks to Mother Teresa for the light she showed to him in the darkness of the Northern Troubles: "Many's the late and lonely night, when exhaustion threatened to induce hopelessness in the struggle to suggest nonviolence for Northern Ireland, that the thought of Mother Teresa's tireless exercise of love in vastly more intimidating circumstances provided energy and strength. I count July 8th 1981, a day of increasing rain and swirling mist, as the most beautiful day of my life. Though I am nervous of Mariology, when Mother Teresa spoke about the presence of Mary at the Crucifixion and asked people not to be bitter, Mary became a powerful and lovable example rather than an obscure and idealised abstraction. When Mother Teresa indicated that the loving presence of the forgiving God was available to everyone, free, one sensed the immediate truth of it, and that this was not the special preserve of persons like herself."

Gone but Not Forgotten

"Where were you the night John F Kennedy was shot?" This was a question I had often heard posed as I was growing up but I never really understood the power of a single event to remain frozen in the memory until Remembrance Sunday, 1987. Even the hardest heart could not but have been melted by Gordon Wilson's intensely moving account of how he lay bleeding under the rubble, clutching his daughter's hand and heard her fading voice saying: "Daddy, I love you very much." Immediately after the carnage caused by an IRA bomb, communal passions threatened to explode. In this highly charged atmosphere Gordon's words of forgiveness diffused an extremely volatile situation.

I met him in Enniskillen years after the death of his daughter. As I sat down he looked me steadfastly in the eye. His own eyes were soft and kind and so being stared at was not threatening for a stranger like myself. Yet he had a disconcerting habit of looking deep into your eyes and then into some unseen mystical place.

We talked about Marie, the child whose birth was

sired by so many dreams and by so much love. He was a man who dedicated his final years to breaking free from the tyranny of the past and trying to put his own troubled past in the perspective of a better future for our troubled island.

Despite the trauma of the Enniskillen bombing Gordon never lost his seeds of faith or hope. On the contrary those virtues blossomed in adversity. Out of the darkness came light. Touching rock bottom he abandoned himself to reach out to the transcendent.

"When you think of my physical sufferings from the bomb, I got away very light. I can cope with it easy enough – it is much more difficult to cope with Marie's loss."

Having entered a new world of suffering and fear without any familiar landmarks in his vulnerability and powerlessness, Gordon experienced total dependence on God. This was not an academic exercise but an authentic human Calvary. Yet Gordon saw in the darkness, physical and emotional, of his condition that God was with him in a very real way, transforming the savage into the sacred.

The physical legacy of that day of the explosion was most evident in the awkward way he tried to light a cigarette. The bomb blast left him with greatly diminished power in one hand. He fought manfully to disguise his annoyance with his incapacity.

My abiding memory of him, though, is of an incident the day we met. As we spoke above his draper's shop in Enniskillen, his two young grand-children burst in the door. His serious face broke into the most magnificent warm smile and his eyes lit up when he saw them. To many people this soft-spoken native of County Leitrim will always be remembered as a man who embodied the Christian virtue of forgiveness. I remember him, though, as I remember my own grandfather, as a man who doted on his grandchildren.

"I believe that for the sake of our children and our grandchildren we can't stay trapped in the past. For too long we have been like prisoners in cells. We must break free and end the 'them and us' mentality. We've got to change our attitudes and our mindsets. People have to understand it is not about negotiating convictions but about walking a path together."

To my surprise Gordon brought up the subject of Mother Teresa in the course of our lengthy conversation:

"Mother Teresa untangles from the sea of dogma a simple message that true religion is about love not hate – about reaching out in handshake and not with clenched fists.

"When I spoke that day I was only speaking for myself. I never envisaged that my words would have the impact they did. If I had time to reflect I would have wanted to be more eloquent but I think the reaction to Mother Teresa shows that people seem to respond better to sincerity than eloquence. Maybe there is an important lesson for us there. Mother Teresa alerts us to the fact that forgiveness and excusing are not simply different but polar opposites. If one was not really to blame, then there is nothing to forgive. To excuse somebody who can really produce good excuses is not Christian charity; it is only fairness. To be a Christian means to forgive the inexcusable, because God has forgiven the inexcusable in us. Excuses by themselves have a minimal value; since by definition they are powerless in the face of the inexcusable and the unjustifiable. Only forgiveness can achieve this. It is only through forgiveness that we are set free for freedom.

"Throughout our history the abuse of religion has brought nothing but division to our troubled country. When Jesus forgave the inexcusable on the cross he showed that Christianity is a potentially healing and unifying force in our society. In his darkest hour, his words of forgiveness showed that the gentleness of Christianity is stronger than a terrorist's bomb.

"Every father thinks that their own daughter is sweeter than everyone else's. I suppose I was no different. I think though she was a very good person. I know that sounds very pious and that kind of language is not fashionable today. I didn't want to contaminate Marie's memory by using dirty talk. Nothing that I could say was going to bring Marie back. I couldn't bring myself to wish hate on the people who killed my daughter. Not everybody understood. I am sad to report that I lost friends because of what I said that day but I did what I thought was right and I am prepared to accept the consequences.

"To be honest I am still shocked about the fuss I created. All I tried to do was to do what Jesus asked. As he hung on the cross, what did he say? *'Father, forgive them, they know not what they do.'* If you are a Christian you have, like Mother Teresa, to at least try and live your life as Jesus asked. I'm not saying that is always easy. In fact a lot of the time it is really hard and I suspect there are days that Mother Teresa must know that too."

Imagine

I probed Mother Teresa about the extent to which Northern Ireland impacted on her everyday thoughts:

"I, my Sisters and our poor are praying for you in Ireland. The whole world is praying that you will open your hearts in love to God. In the name of God and in the name of your people do not destroy life and peace. Let your names be remembered for the good you have done, the joy you have spread and the love you have shared.

"I would ask people in Ireland to pray for me and my Sisters as we try to love and serve the poor because they belong to God and are loved in His eyes – so we and our poor are praying for you. We pray that you will love and nourish what God has so lovingly entrusted into your care. I ask people in Ireland to be aware that:

> *The fruit of silence is prayer*
> *The fruit of prayer is faith*
> *The fruit of faith is love*
> *The fruit of love is service*
> *The fruit of service is peace."*

Mother Teresa had a direct message for the men of violence:

"Pray with me. Together I would ask them to join me and say:

> *Lead me from death to life*
> *From falsehood to truth*
> *Lead me from despair to hope*
> *From fear to truth*
> *Lead me from hate to love*
> *From war to peace*
> *Let peace fill our hearts*
> *Our world our universe*
> *Peace peace peace.*

"Then I would ask them to join me in the prayer of peace written by St Francis of Assisi, which we say each day. It is a reminder of how we can create peace in our lives by giving ourselves, with an open and clean heart, to others:

Lord, make me a channel of Thy peace
That where there is hatred, I may bring love;
That where there is wrong, I may bring the spirit
  of forgiveness;
That where there is discord, I may bring harmony;
That where there is error, I may bring truth;
That where there is doubt, I may bring faith;
That where there is despair, I may bring hope;
That where there are shadows, I may bring light;
That where there is sadness, I may bring joy.
Lord, grant that I may seek rather to comfort than
  to be comforted,
To understand than to be understood;
To love than to be loved.
For it is by forgetting self that one finds;
It is by forgiving that one is forgiven;
It is by dying that one awakens to eternal life.

"Prayer makes your heart bigger, until it is capable of containing the gift of God Himself. I believe that politicians spend too little time on their knees. I am convinced that they would be better politicians if they were to do so. There are some people who, in order not to pray, use as an excuse the fact that life is so hectic that it prevents them from praying. This cannot be. Prayer does not demand that we interrupt our work, but that we continue working as if it were a prayer. It is not necessary to always be meditating nor to consciously experience the sensation that we are talking to God, no matter how nice this would be. What matters is being with him, living in him, in his will. To love with a pure heart, to love everybody, is a twenty-four-hour prayer."

I wondered if she was optimistic about the prospect of peace in Northern Ireland in her lifetime:

"Yesterday is gone. Tomorrow has not yet come. We have only today. Let us begin. Make us, Lord, worthy to serve our brothers and sisters who are scattered all over the world, who die and live alone and poor. Give them today, using our hands, their daily bread. And, using our love, give them peace and happiness.

"Love one another as God loves each of you. Jesus came to give us the good news that God loves us and that He wants us to love one another. And when the time comes to die and go home to God we will be welcomed in love.

"One of my favourite readings is from Chapter 13 of Paul's letter to the Corinthians: '*Love is always patient and kind; love is never jealous; love is not boastful or conceited; it is never rude and never seeks its own advantage, it does not take offence or store up grievances. Love does not rejoice at wrongdoing, but finds its joy in the truth. It is always ready to make allowances, to trust, to hope and to endure whatever comes. Love never comes to an end.*' Love is unending because love is undying.

"Some people are hard to love sometimes. Remember that everybody has something good inside them. Some hide it, some neglect it, but it is always there.

"God has been so good to us: works of love are always a means of becoming closer to God. Look at what Jesus did in His life on earth. Love until it hurts. If it hurts, then it'll be better because of it. We must grow in love and to do this we must go on loving and loving and giving and giving until it hurts – just like Jesus did. All of us need to do ordinary things with extraordinary love: little things like caring for the sick and all the lonely people. We all must give something that will cost us. It is easy to give what you can live without. It is only when we give what we can't live without or don't want to live without that our gift becomes a sacrifice. Any sacrifice is useful if it is done out of love. This giving until it hurts is what I call love in action and what I would like to see most in Ireland.

"I was once walking down the street and a beggar came to me and said: 'Mother Teresa, everybody's giving to you, I also want to give to you. Today I got just a few small coins and I want to give them to you.' I thought for a second because if I took them he would have nothing to eat tonight, but if I didn't take them I would hurt his feelings. So I put out my hands and I took the money. I have never seen such joy on anybody's face as I saw on his – that a beggar, he too, could give to Mother Teresa. It was a big sacrifice for him because it was all he had. It was beautiful. It was such a tiny amount that I could do nothing with it, but as he gave it up and I took it, it became like a fortune because it was given with so much love. So my message to the people of Ireland is love until it hurts, because in that way we become capable of loving more deeply, more beautifully, more wholly humanly. God loves people who give joyfully and, if you give joyfully, you always give more. A joyful heart is the result of a heart burning with love. Works of love are always works of joy. We don't need to look for happiness: if we have love for others we'll be given it. It is the gift of God."

Mother Teresa was a big admirer of people who loved until it hurt. One stood out for her. On March 24th 1980 the Archbishop of San Salvador was reading the Gospel: *"The hour is coming for the son of man to be glorified . . . unless the grain of wheat falls to the earth and dies, it remains only a grain. But if it dies it bears much fruit."* Only minutes before a bullet from an assassin's rifle tore through his chest, because he had forcefully spoken out against the repressive policies of the government, Oscar Romero preached on the gospel he had just read: "Whoever, out of love of Christ, gives himself to the service of others, will live like the grain of wheat that dies and only apparently dies. If it did not die, it would remain alone. Only in giving ourselves totally, can we produce a harvest."

Mother Teresa believed that such sacrificial love was needed if peace was ever to come to Northern Ireland:

"Works of love are always works of peace. Whenever you share love with others, you'll notice that peace comes to you and to them. When there is peace, there is God. That is how God touches our lives and shows His love for us by pouring peace and joy into our hearts.

"It is not enough to say I love God, but I do not love my neighbour. St John says you are a liar if you say you love God and you do not love your neighbour. How can you love God whom you do not see, if you do not love your neighbour whom you see, whom you touch, with whom you live? And this is very important for us to realise – that love, to be true, has to hurt. It hurt Jesus to love us, it hurt him.

"Keep the joy of loving God in your heart and share this joy with all you meet especially your family. That is the path to peace.

"*People are often unreasonable, irrational, and self-centred. Forgive them anyway.*

If you are kind, people may accuse you of selfish, ulterior motives. Be kind anyway.

If you are successful, you will win some unfaithful friends and some genuine enemies. Succeed anyway.

If you are honest and sincere people may deceive you. Be honest and sincere anyway.

What you spend years creating, others could destroy overnight. Create anyway.

If you find serenity and happiness, some may be jealous. Be happy anyway.

The good you do today, will often be forgotten.

Do good anyway.

Give the best you have, and it will never be enough. Give your best anyway.

In the final analysis, it is between you and God. It was never between you and them anyway."

Chapter 5

For God's Sake

The Sufi story of the ferryman who was taking a
learned theologian across the water provided a
cautionary tale for Mother Teresa about cerebral
theological reflection. The theologian was explaining
the importance of using the attributes of God and of
studying the divine philosophy for the salvation of
the soul. The ferryman, a simple man, admitted that
these great things were way beyond him. Then he
suddenly said to the theologian: "Can you swim?"
The theologian admitted he couldn't. "Which is a pity,"
said the ferryman "because the boat is sinking."

Paralysis by analysis was never a danger for Mother
Teresa and her Sisters. Sometimes their work brought
her to dangerous places but her philosophy was: "The
one who kneels to the Lord can stand up to
anything."

She waved her hand dismissively when I asked her if she was ever afraid:

"No, I have given my life to God. Once we were going to go to Sudan with food. There was a danger of shooting. Five of us signed a document that we were ready to die if the plane was shot down. The next day when we were to leave there was a threat to shoot down the plane. The pilot refused to go. Otherwise we would have certainly gone."

Knowing that the secret of success is consistency of purpose, from the outset Mother Teresa saw the value of collaborating with other agencies to offer the maximum amount of assistance to the poor. This collaborative process led her to form many fruitful partnerships with Irish aid agencies who work hand in hand with local people on the ground to build a new future out of a very troubled past. Historically many missionaries who worked so hard for so long on the missions to the developing world shared a wonderful commitment to serve. In more recent times, though, lay people have taken up the torch.

I wondered why this Irish connection had been so prominent in Mother Teresa's projects in the developing world:

"Some of my Sisters work in Australia. On a reservation, among the Aborigines, there was an elderly man. I can assure you that you have never seen a situation as difficult as that poor old man's. He was completely ignored by everyone. His home was disordered and dirty.

"I told him, 'Please, let me clean your house, wash your clothes, and make your bed.'

"He answered, 'I'm okay like this. Let it be.'

"I said again, 'You will be still better if you allow me to do it.'

"He finally agreed. So I was able to clean his house and wash his clothes. I discovered a beautiful lamp, covered with dust. Only God knows how many years since he last lit it.

"I said to him, 'Don't you light your lamp? Don't you ever use it?'

"He answered, 'No. No one comes to see me. I have no need to light it. Who would I light it for?'

"I asked, 'Would you light it every night if the Sisters came?'

"He replied, 'Of course.'

"From that day on the Sisters committed themselves to visiting him every evening. We cleaned the lamp, and the Sisters would light it every evening.

"Two years passed. I had completely forgotten that man. Then he sent this message: 'Tell my friend that the light she lit in my life continues to shine still.'

"One of my clearest memories of our work in Calcutta is when late in the day, around ten at night, the doorbell rang. I opened the door and found a man shivering from the cold. 'Mother Teresa, I heard that you just received an important prize. When I heard this I decided to offer you something too. Here, you have it: this is what I collected today.' It was little, but in his case it was everything. I was more moved by what he did than by the Nobel Prize.

"I thought these were both very small things. Since my time in Rathfarnham I know that the Irish understand the importance of small things and these Irish aid workers understand that the poor don't care how much you know until they know that you care.

"Because of your history you know that if we worry too much about ourselves, we won't have time for others. Once I received a beautiful letter and a sizable donation from an Italian child who had just made his First Communion. In his letter he explained that before he made his First Communion, he had asked his parents not to buy him a special suit, nor to have a party to celebrate the occasion. And he also said he had told his relatives and friends not to give him any gifts. He would give everything up in exchange for the money they would have spent in order to send it to Mother Teresa. It was a beautiful demonstration of generosity by that child. All over the world I have seen such an ability to sacrifice, to deprive themselves of something, in Irish aid workers.

"I feel that we are in such a hurry that we do not even have time to look at one another and smile. Today it is very fashionable to talk about the poor. Unfortunately, it is not fashionable to talk with them. The Irish aid workers, though, reach out to the desolation of the poor – not only their material poverty but also their spiritual wounds as well. They know the best way of satisfying our bretheren's hunger is to share with them whatever we have – to share with them until we ourselves feel what they feel because the poor do not need our condescending attitude or our pity but our love and tenderness. They also know that the less we have, the more we give. It seems absurd but it's the logic of love. When they place themselves at the service of the poor, it causes an authentic revolution, the biggest, the most difficult one: the revolution of love. True love causes pain. Jesus, in order to give us the proof of his love, died on the cross. A mother, in order to give birth to her baby, has to suffer. If you really love one another, you will not be able to avoid making sacrifices.

"Jesus became a child to teach us to love God. In the eyes of the child, I see the spirit of life, of God. What we say does not matter, only what God says through us. The poor call to us. We have to be aware of them in order to love them. We have to ask ourselves if we know the truth. Those Irish aid workers know this. If there were poor on the moon, they would go there too. They know that the poor are precisely the ones who better understand human dignity. If they have a problem, it is not lack of money, but the fact that their right to be treated humanely and with tenderness is not recognised. Good works are like links that form a chain of love.

"They also know that we have to keep going. To keep a lamp burning we have to keep putting oil in it."

Calcutta 1980

As the driving engine of GOAL, one of Ireland's most important relief agencies working in the developing world, John O'Shea is probably the best known figure in the world of development aid in Ireland. Like Mother Teresa the energy cell of his personality was quite clearly singed by his own perceptions of poverty in India. In sympathy with those in suffering, he is ruthlessly objective in his critique of the system which makes them suffer. A visit to Calcutta gave him new insights. His mind is a theatre of memories of the trip – the memory bank of his instincts has displaced the casual paraphernalia of trivia to their rightful place. He retains very strong memories of his first meeting with Mother Teresa:

"The Mass in a small church hidden amid Calcutta's slums began at 4.30 a.m, but I felt obliged to be there on time. Promised a lift with the Missionaries of Charity to a leper colony in Tanager, some three hours outside the city, I felt that joining them in prayer as the day began was the least I could do. The Mass over, I hung around the yard outside, waiting for my lift and wondering what an Irish sports journalist could discuss with an Indian nun for three hours in a car. I needn't have worried. My companion for the journey was Mother Teresa, and I spent the rest of the day in awe, watching this small woman who had enough love for everyone she met.

"The day was thirty years ago but it had a lasting effect on me. It was my first trip to Calcutta, and surrounded by what seemed to be an unending tide of misery, I began to despair.

"In the nightmare of Calcutta's slums, it seemed as if the only release was death. Sickened by the sight of so much poverty, I approached Mother Teresa. 'When you work in these conditions every day, surrounded by so much suffering,' I said, 'do you ever stop and wonder if you're making an impact on this poverty?'

"She turned to me and smiled, saying: 'Every day of my life in Calcutta, I make it my business to lift a leper or a dying person or a child in desperate need and hug and kiss that person. I don't know whether that it is the best thing to do for that person but I do know it's the right thing to do.'

"Years later, I still feel privileged at the opportunity I had that day. Amid the dirt and the dying in Calcutta's slums, in the depths of the most appalling poverty, I witnessed the power of love, and its ability to light up even the darkest places.

"The greatest thing she did was inspire people to do things. Like Nelson Mandela and Aung San Suu Kyi she had the greatest prestige that any leader could carry: the designation of "peacemaker".

"I became good friends with Mother and had great discussions with her. She was less than five-foot tall but tough. That day I got the lift with her the authorities were thinking of moving the leper colony to the other side of the road. I couldn't understand what she was saying, but she won. She got her own way."

The House of Angels

Mother Teresa's hope was often challenged – never more so than when she heard of the devastating famine in Ethiopia in 1984. Knowing that you cannot discover new oceans unless you have the courage to lose sight of the shore, she felt she had no option but to visit the scene for herself. What she saw would have shocked the hardest heart.

Bloated bellies and matchstick limbs were the order of the day. Entire families were left shaking in the heat of the midday sun, too tired to respond to coaxing because they were in an advanced stage of starvation. Children's ribs stuck through their skins. A few were still able to smile even though they were covered in filth and scabs and there was swelling under their eyes.

Their chat was smothered by a more incessant sound, the sound of coughing. Many were barely able to walk and needed a stick to lean on. Mothers were very distressed as they cradled their children. In the village there were tiny children no bigger than one would expect a new-born baby to be, even though they were two or three years old.

Some had lost their homes and were searching for somewhere to lay their weary heads at night. They simply carried their few belongings in a bag over their shoulders. The series of human tragedies was evident in the tears, the heavily lined faces, the letters to loved ones that can never be written and the aching hearts for those gone to their eternal reward. Faces were bruised and swollen – young people looked old. People who had joked and laughed and who were full of the joys of life were suddenly transformed into creatures of fear. It is impossible to describe the tension, the fear, the concern people had for their families.

At the height of the crisis so many corpses littered the roads and fields that the survivors no longer bothered to move them, unless they were relatives or friends. Some had planned for it by climbing under their reed mats to die so that others could tie them up more easily. In this vision of hell, at night the living and dead lay together. When the stench of rotting flesh hung in the air a grim-faced aid worker spread disinfectant over the dead ones and wrapped their faces in scarves and rags and surgical masks, hoping to filter the stench from the rotting bodies. It was as if the very ground was infected by the dying.

A relentless stream of people, bathed in golden

sunshine, had to weave their way down to the waterpoint with anything that could hold water. The search for clean water yielded nothing, only a thick, slimy brew so fouled by human waste so that it did more to spread disease than quench thirst. A score of men, women and children sat in silent expectation around the food tent – a few had their hands out in supplication. They were destined for a disappointment. There was no food until the morning. One of the children frantically sought out a grain of spilled rice from the dust on the ground. Bliss would be biscuits and rehydration salts.

For miles around, the trees had been disappearing, fed into pitiful cooking fires. One corner of the camp was assigned for the dead. They lay in neat rows; some had their mouths ajar after what had been a painful end. When the weather hotted up some of the corpses began to bloat and burst. The children died the quickest in this latter-day slaughter of the innocents. It was always the weakest who lost out.

One little girl was getting special treatment. She was rescued from being buried alive when she was noticed moving amongst a pile of corpses tossed into the mass grave.

Mother Teresa's Sisters were grossly understaffed, had inadequate equipment and medicines and were working in the worst possible circumstances as part of a reactive relief effort fighting first to contain and then to control the epidemics in this human tragedy. This illiterate, chiefly rural, population's most basic wish was a good meal for themselves and the surviving members of their family. A round-the-clock service was provided lest disease and starvation exact a toll that even the most savage soldiers could not. Mother Teresa leaned over a young boy running a high fever and wiped flies from swollen eyes. His eyes were empty, waterless like the rest of his body, and they could not find a vein to insert the intravenous tube that could save him. The force of love, of unexpected and invigorating innocence, moved Mother Teresa deeply.

With dying families too weak to look after themselves, evidence of neglect was everywhere. Some people, too weak to walk or stumble for water, drank their own urine. There was no room for optimism. Lethargy had induced a permanent premature state of rigor mortis. In winter bodies lay frozen in the mud. Innocence was shattered for evermore. The sound of wailing women boomed all around like field-guns on a battlefield with only intermittent moments of deafening silence. A landscape once virgin pure lay shattered like a broken bottle. The assembly line of victims was unending.

Fear was the only real sign of life, as beauty and goodness, like most people in the area, died slowly in agony. To the embattled, emotionally bankrupt and hopelessly disorganised, the ordinary joys and sorrows were an irrelevance. The chances of survival were slim. For many, death was a welcome escape from pain and heartache. The afterlife was the only dream they could still cherish. For the strong, life was a victory over death. There were so many others, good people, kind, affectionate, hard-working but bone-weary, without a bite to eat. They were the un-rememberables.

Ethiopia took a hold of Mother Teresa's imagination as it was an enduring monument to inhumanity, ineffectiveness and indifference. It opened questions, often violently, about her history and identity and even went further to some secret compass points which steered her to somewhere she did not know. As she walked by the field she tried to listen to its secrets of lives gained and lives lost, strange riches and sadness. This modern-day Calvary had a music of its own. The notes which entered her consciousness were notes of loneliness, poignant cries of quiet despair. In her mind people long dead lived again, somehow speaking to years that belong to people not yet born. This new incarnation of Calvary crossed boundaries where sadness and pain met so dramatically.

As an eyewitness to such horrendous tragedy she believed she had a duty to work for justice for those too weak to help themselves despite the lack of facilities. Amputations were often carried out without anaesthetic. Doctors managed because they had to manage. For old people it was the worst. They saw everything they had worked for destroyed. It was incredibly tough to see the place they had been born and bred in turned into a giant cemetery. Life was not really life for many of them. There was no living, just existence:

"The Prime Minister of Ethiopia told me, 'Even though we might have to expel all missionaries we will not allow your Sisters to leave because I am told, and I have checked it myself to be true, that you truly love the poor and take care of them.'"

The Irish aid agency Ethiopiaid has been working with Mother Teresa's Missionaries of Charity in Addis Ababa, Ethiopia, since 1993, where a group of nuns run a compound known affectionately as "The House of Angels". Their constituency ranks among the most desperate on earth and nobody is turned away. The Sisters run an orphanage for children who have lost their parents, many of them to HIV/AIDS. Often the children themselves are infected with HIV too and many do not survive beyond their teens.

Caroline Swann manager of Ethiopiaid Ireland explains: "Their [the Missionaries of Charity's] work at the 'House of Angels' is one of our most popular partners and donors often ask for more information about them. They don't turn anyone away from their hospice and have many patients – from those receiving palliative care to others who require respite from the hardships of a life on the streets. I received a brief report from a trustee of Ethiopiaid in the UK who went there in November 2009. He and his wife were moved by what they saw – there were over a thousand people there with only three volunteers beyond the Sisters. He felt they were doing an extraordinary job in very difficult circumstances. We will definitely be continuing to support them."

One person with a unique insight into this work is an Irish Jesuit priest, Dr Michael O'Sullivan. He is head of Theological Studies at All Hallows College, Dublin, and has extensive experience living and working with disadvantaged people in Ireland, Latin America and East Africa:

"I visited a centre in Ethiopia once where Mother Teresa's Sisters were caring for people in dire need and was overwhelmed by the suffering I saw, and deeply humbled by the amazing commitment of the Sisters. Mother Teresa lived with such suffering day by day, year after year. She lived with it even when travelling because of her interiority which kept it close to her. It should not surprise us, therefore, to learn after her death that she lived with dreadful desolation, for how could it be otherwise? Like Jesus on the cross she lived an eclipse of God, only for much longer. And yet God was there all the time, there in her heart with its courage to love beyond belief."

Mother Teresa also decided to focus on one of the most compelling challenges to our world imaginable. The emergence of any new disease inevitably provokes fear; however, the rapid spread of AIDS, its transmissible nature and its medical complexity exacerbated the normal problems and tensions associated with a new disease.

Mother Teresa went to Africa as it was the place with the highest incidence of AIDS. She got the opportunity to engage with the subject in an emotionally significant and humanising way. The agonising tyranny of the plight of the victims of AIDS inspired Mother Teresa to do something positive.

Her Sisters shared an approach to community development in the developing world pioneered by Paolo Freire, whose experiences in South America made him acutely aware of the attitudes of the would-be "helpers" towards those who were seen to be in need of "help". Often there was a conviction about the unassailable worth of some intervention and the benefits it would confer. Freire characterises this as "cultural invasion", the starting point being the world of the "helpers" from which they view and enter the world of those they invade. This is in contrast to "cultural synthesis" where those who come from another world do not do so as invaders but as partners. This is the road the Missionaries of Charity has chosen. The challenge they face today is to recover the "listening" character of good missionary activity, to educate in an ongoing conversation, and to find God in the margins and voices previously ignored. The possibility for enrichment in this listening process is enormous.

Their lives' work seems to be an attempt to live an old prayer:

God be in my head and in my understanding;
God be in mine eyes, and in my looking;
God be in my mouth and in my speaking;
God be in my heart, and in my thinking;
God be at mine end, and my departing.

In the intermingling of faith and life they want to be attentive to where God is today. They are searching for a way to live that is authentic and which offers an alternative to an individualistic way of life which is increasingly prevalent in the modern world. In responding to the needs of society they are striving to bear witness to Christ and to reveal His love to the struggling people.

Mother Teresa's contacts with Ethiopia would bring her into contact with an unlikely Irishman.

The Odd Couple

Having sprung to fame in the 1970s when his band the Boomtown Rats had a string of hits, most famously "I Don't Like Mondays", Bob Geldof became a global superstar in 1984 when he devised and organised the Band-Aid record "Let them Know It's Christmas" to alleviate the plight of the starving millions in Ethiopia. The following year his fame reached even further dizzy heights when he ran the phenomenally successful Live-Aid concerts. In January 1985 he was in Addis Ababa when he saw Mother Teresa.

Photographers fell over themselves to grab pictures of this unlikely conversation – particularly given Geldof's penchant for swearing. The media had a field day with the story, dubbing them "The Saint and The Sinner".

Although born into a Catholic family and educated by the Holy Ghost Fathers in Ireland's most famous rugby nursery Blackrock College, Geldof had long since renounced his Catholicism. In his 1980 hit "Banana Republic" he had rubbished the influence of priests in Irish society. Yet by a delicious irony of history Geldof, with his Irish Catholic schooling, became the best-known secular equivalent of the work of Irish missionaries, bringing the same sort of almost missionary zeal to the task. His message of giving until it hurts was remarkably similar to Mother Teresa's – apart from the various expletives he used to stress the urgency of the situation. Both had the same stubborn natures, the same flair for spotting PR opportunities and getting the most out of them, the same apparent indifference to their appearance and both were incredibly resilient.

In his 1986 autobiography *Is That It?* Geldof recalled his impressions of her. His first thought was how tiny she looked and then that she was a "battered, wizened woman". Somewhat surprisingly he was then very taken by her feet. He noticed that while her habit was clean and well-cared-for her sandals were simply "beaten-up pieces of leather from which her feet protruded, gnarled and misshapen as old tree roots". When Sir Bob bent to kiss her, as it seemed the polite thing to do, he was caught off guard when she bowed her head so quickly that he had no option but to kiss "the top of her wimple". Geldof went on to tell her about when his band had played in India and offered to play a concert for her mission. She declined his offer immediately as she did not need such activities because God would provide.

Geldof proceeded to illustrate the way in which God would provide.

At their first meeting at an official function, while the television cameras were rolling, she grabbed the chance to say that she had observed on her way from the airport some palatial old buildings which seemed unoccupied and wanted to know if she could have them as orphanages. A government minister who formed the centrepiece of the official delegation, seeking some media attention and with an eye for a photo opportunity, was brought into the discussion. He tried to kick for touch but, unable to say no on live television, he eventually conceded that he would try to find her a suitable home for an orphanage. Quick as a flash Mother Teresa said: "Two orphanages." Through gritted teeth he agreed: "Two orphanages."

Geldof remarked that the instant he met Mother Teresa she struck him as "being the living embodiment of moral good". He went on to comment that there was nothing "otherworldly or divine about her". His considered verdict was: "The way she spoke to the journalists showed her to be as deft a manipulator of media as any high-powered American PR expert. She does a sort of 'Oh dear, I'm just a frail old lady' schtick. She was outrageously brilliant. There was no false modesty about her and there was a certainty of purpose which left her little patience. But she was totally selfless; every moment her aim seemed to be, how can I see this or that situation to help others?"

Try Hard

Over a decade after her death Mother Teresa's Sisters continue to collaborate with a variety of organisations, like The Ireland Fund of Japan which has assisted the Missionaries of Charity to feed between 400 and 600 homeless people daily near Ueno in Tokyo.

I wondered what Mother Teresa herself thought about the work of these Irish agencies:

"Often I think God is absent from my life and my work. I wonder if I am doing any good at all. At times I feel the only thing I can do is show mercy. St Vincent de Paul told us to always turn our eyes from the study of your own sin to the contemplation of God's mercy and asked us to devote much more thought to his great love for us than our unworthiness towards Him. We need to focus on His strength rather than our weakness. When we do this and surrender ourselves to God's love in the hope that He will make us what He requires us to be, He will bless all that the Irish aid workers do even when they too feel they are going through dark days."

When asked if she would like Irish development agencies to help her more in her work, Mother Teresa shook her head firmly: "God does not expect people in Ireland to do my work for me. God wants them to do their work with a good heart as well as they can."

Chapter 6

An Iconic Figure

Mother Teresa had a profound influence on the Irish consciousness. The first time I became fully aware of that was on the annual pilgrimage to Croagh Patrick, in County Mayo.

We arrived at the little bridge in Murrish on the Louisburgh-Westport road. The first thing I heard was an entrepreneur shouting "Sticks for the Reek! Sticks for the Reek!" as he sought to sell walking sticks to help pilgrims negotiate the hazardous mountain. Although many were climbing in their bare feet, we were attired in hobnailed boots and light rain-gear. We joined the stream of people on the 2510-foot vertical, after a three-mile walk around the hill and up the "Cásán Phádraic" known locally as "the ladder".

We began at midnight and started climbing in the

darkness, beaconed upwards by a magical river of transitory flash-lamps which led past the lighthouses of the vendors' tents. There was plenty of good-natured banter from the pilgrims and extensive analysis of the state of Connacht football. "Will Roscommon bate Kerry?" "Mayo's forwards lost it for them this year." "Galway have never replaced the Terrible Twins."

I thought we had reached the top when we came to a short plateau but it was only an intermediary stop. However, the cool fanning breeze coming across the open mountain revived my drooping spirits. An eternity later we finally made it to the summit. I had a powerful sense of anti-climax on arrival. It was clouded, obscuring the magnificent view of the land and bay that I had expected.

As I was parched with the thirst I was delighted when a complete stranger, wearing a saffron and blue Clare jersey, handed me a bottle of water. When I went to thank him he just waved my words away and to my astonishment quoted Mother Teresa's words: *"I ask you to do one thing: do not tire of giving. Give until it hurts, until you feel the pain."* A small farmer, he had a deep devotion to Mother Teresa and not for the first time I wondered why this tiny woman could inspire such feelings of attachment from so many Irish people.

I knew that in part it was as a consequence of her being such a source of fascination to many in the Irish media throughout her lifetime. She was memorably interviewed by Gay Byrne on the *Late, Late Show*. Given the centrality of the programme in Irish life, it provided Mother Teresa with the perfect platform to capture the hearts and minds of a huge swathe of the Irish population. Gay subsequently described her as one of the interviewees who made the most impression because of the wall of certainty her faith seemed to give her.

In December 1990, during one of his many visits to Ireland, I interviewed Cliff Richard who provided me with a revealing insight into Mother Teresa's willingness to accommodate the media:

"I met Mother Teresa just once. In 1976 I interviewed her in India for the charity Tearfund about her work with the destitute and dying. It was a powerful experience to meet such an icon. I remember we were all very amused when we arrived at the door to her hospice, which was down a tiny alley, to find one of those old-fashioned name-boards with a piece of wood which you slide from left to right to indicate whether someone is 'In' or 'Out'. There were a whole lot of names but among them we found 'Mother Teresa'. She was then in her late sixties, a frail, hunched little figure.

"She was awe-inspiring but also delightful. She introduced us to some of her fellow nuns – all dressed as she was – and showed us around; she showed us the holy area where they prayed, and the area where the people came in off the streets, many of them on stretchers. She was hugging the patients as we passed them, saying, 'These are sweet people and when they die they will know that we have loved them.' That was her premise, that no one should die alone and unloved; everyone should live with dignity.

"After the tour of the hospice, I interviewed her, and then – I had my guitar as usual – we all sang and then we prayed together. In the car on the way back to our hotel at the end of the day, someone said, 'Let's listen to the tape.' So we put the tape into the machine, pressed 'play' – and nothing happened. We turned it over: nothing. We tried every inch of it: there wasn't a single syllable to be heard. As soon as we got back to the hotel I rang Mother Teresa and said, 'I'm so sorry to have to ask you this but would it be possible for us to come back?'

"'Why?' she said. 'What happened?'

"I said, 'There's nothing on the tape.'

"Her reply was simple: 'Okay, something you said or I said must have displeased Jesus. He wiped the tape. You'd better come back. We'll do it again.'

"Mother Teresa could not have been more gracious and I thought, no matter how much we make people icons, a part of them has to remain real, and she was one hundred per cent real.

"I came away thinking, why do we complicate our faith? Why do we have to intellectualise everything? Sometimes the intellect clouds the issue. For Mother Teresa, it was simple: one of us said something that

Jesus didn't like, so come back and we'll put it right. Second time around, the recording was perfect, and it was the same tape. I would have said it was the same interview too, but maybe not."

Thy Kingdom Come

In 1958 the Catholic Church underwent a major shift when an Italian peasant's son became Pope John XXIII. The smiling pope realised that his Church was standing still in the middle of a changing world. In 1962 he brought the bishops of the Church together to meet him in Rome, the first time this had been done in nearly a century. The Second Vatican Council made many changes in the way the Catholic Church operated. The winds of change were blowing but many were unhappy with the changes.

The anthem for the 1960's generation was "hope I die before I get old". Theirs was the generation which saw an unprecedented departure from previous generations. It was in the '60s that life as we know it today was shaped and moulded. It was the decade of the Beatles, pirate radio, monster peace-concerts, flower power and Mary Quant. Hope and idealism were the common currency. Nostalgically everything about the time seems good: the concern for peace, the socially concerned songs of Bob Dylan and Joan Baez, and the sense of freedom and optimism.

Higher educational standards, greater foreign

travel and industrialisation opened the windows of change on Irish society. However, the greatest agent of social transformation was unquestionably the emergence of television when topics which had hitherto been shrouded in a veil of secrecy were openly discussed for the first time in pubs and parlours.

New Year's Day 1962 was a watershed in Irish society when Ireland got its first television service. The first television sets began to trickle into homes a few months later. They were the latest of the never-ending miracles of science, those "picture boxes" installed by the wealthier farmers. They held children from their play and adults from their memories beside the fireside. The poorer families, who could not initially afford televisions, would almost beg to spend their evenings in those fortunate houses where the images flickered and came and went. The tenth commandment *"Thou shalt not covet thy neighbour's goods"* had never been broken so often once the televisions came to the country.

The late Dominican priest, Fergal O'Connor, became a household name as a result of being a provocative panellist for many years on *The Late Late Show*. From near Causeway, County Kerry, he was a legendary lecturer in political philosophy in UCD, a social activist from 1962 until his death in 2005, and a campaigner who founded and for several decades directed Sherrard House, a hostel for homeless girls in Dublin, and ALLY, an organisation supporting single mothers. It is difficult to explain the impact of this "liberal priest" on what was a largely conservative country at the time. In Fergal's story we see in microcosm the story of a fast-changing Ireland and the story of how the Church went through profound and often uncomfortable change in the aftermath of the Second Vatican Council.

He recognised that the arrogance of the past needed to give way to humility and that the desire to preach needed to be matched by a willingness to genuinely listen. Above all he understood that people would no longer be lectured to by those who did not know what their real problems were. He believed that the Church must expect rigorous criticism in the intellectual marketplace for some of its positions. He understood instinctively that it would be in the Church's own interest too if it took a less hostile stance to its internal critics in particular and recognised that such criticism is motivated by love, and is not cynical or global but is trying to identify specific areas where corrective surgery is required.

His take on Mother Teresa was characteristically unique:

"I know the popular perception is the archetypal conservative Catholic because of her views on issues like abortion. Yet what amazes me is that so many people have failed to see how modern and radical Mother Teresa was in so many ways. She pioneered the creation of smaller religious communities, more conducive to deeper dialogue, greater sharing of life and vision and the possibility of exploring in greater depth the search for community in today's world.

"She saw religious vows more in terms of possibilities than prohibitions. No longer are they understood as personal means to perfection but as an articulation of the ideals to which all people aspire. Celibacy is now understood as growth in living relationships with God and people transcending the exclusiveness of marital love; poverty is part of the universal desire to share equally and generously the goods of creation; and obedience a deep listening and generous response to the call of life in today's world.

"In the Gospel we find Jesus repeating over and over again the simple advice '*Watch and pray*'. This was not merely a readiness for unexpected death. It is far wider than that. It is to be alert to the call of God in one's immediate situation. The one thread of unity between the Sisters who have followed her and Mother Teresa is that they have all been motivated by the love of Christ. As the old tree of established structures is dying, it is not easy to discern how to graft anew to the future vine. At the moment Mother Teresa's Sisters are at an in-between time in their history, caught between a rich tradition and an as yet unformed new direction. The only thing that can be said with certainty in an uncertain time is that the Sisters will continue to be inspired by the love of Christ. All the old absolutes and certitudes melted away after Vatican II. The familiar black and white gave way to a breathtaking proliferation of grey. Like many communities and congregations she and her Sisters made real efforts to respond to the call of the Second Vatican Council, experiencing a deepening of their faith and commitment and discovering a new joy and fulfilment in their vocation. Mother Teresa represented the church in miniature, a sacrament of Christ's healing presence among people.

"For the first half of the twentieth century, religious became fossilised in admirable institutions of impeccable pedigree which encased them in a cocoon of continuity glorified with the term of tradition. After Vatican II this archaic paternalism was finally consigned to the dustbin, allowing for a new understanding of obedience to emerge. True obedience demands reflection and personal responsibility. The Council brought religious face to face with the problems and inadequacies of the old system. What was not so clear was what should be put in its place. Women congregations in particular were bombarded with advice about how to cope with these changes.

"An influential work at this time was Cardinal Suenens' *The Nun in the World*. His book represented a plea for adaptation of the customs and usages in "active" religious congregations, so as to better meet contemporary needs. He argued that women have a role – *'for better and worse'* – which was not theirs before *'feminine emancipation'*. In the modern world they are wanted, accepted, effective in every sphere of life but the nun had not kept in line with her sister in the world. Loving Christ meant *'loving Him in His living Church in the here and now'*. This involved greater rapport with the world and required that the nun be better informed and au fait with current thought. Changes – not affecting the essence of religious life – were necessary, the central place of prayer in the life of the nun was restated but *'redundant devotions must be mercilessly eliminated'*. A re-assessment and possible pruning of the duties nuns were involved in was called for.

"In 1962 nobody batted an eyelid that a man should take it on himself to write a blueprint for nuns. After two millennia of Christianity, Christian women still had apparently to fight for equality despite the fact that the Gospels clearly demonstrate that Christ's sisters were just as fully his disciples as were his brothers. The feminist awakening has had a major impact on religious women. For most of their history they were conditioned to think of themselves as less important than their male counterparts and to accept that fact without much question. Mother Teresa endorsed the move towards insertion in local society because of its valuing of intimacy and companionship on the common human journey.

"The most obvious external manifestation of the Sisters' new relationship with the world was their clothing. Sisters had started to modify their dress even before Vatican II but they had to obtain a special dispensation from the Holy See on each occasion. This led to the ludicrous situation of a Superior General coming before Cardinal Antoniutto of the "appropriate Pontifical Commission" with the slightly modified habit, modelled by a younger nun, and awaiting for a magisterial "yes" or "no" as the *will of God*. The gross arrogance of men deciding what women should wear almost defies comprehension. However, feminism was only one of the forces for change in women's congregations.

"Nursing Sisters were the butt of many jokes from their patients about their new dress. One Sister who had removed her veil was told by one patient: 'I never thought you had hair.' She responded by asking: 'What did you think I had? Feathers?' Another Sister faced with a similar situation responded by, in sporting parlance, turning defence into attack: 'Sister, can I ask you a personal question?' the patient asked. 'Certainly.' 'Did anyone ever tell you that you were beautiful?' 'Yes. Can I ask you a personal question?' 'You may.' 'Did your bowels move today?'

"Some Sisters tried to get into the spirit of Vatican II, to literally be 'open to the outside world' by learning to drive which led to moments of high comedy. One elderly superior who was learning her motoring skills liked to take a younger Sister with her for moral support. The younger women found this a hazardous experience and resorted to all kinds of creative ways to avoid being recruited as co-pilots. Their most common tactic was to hide in the confessional box.

"Mother Teresa was ahead of the Council insofar as she was not hugely concerned with rules and regulations. Energy was released to respond to the call to justice and love for the poor which found such a ready echo in the hearts of religious women. Mother Teresa recognised that the seclusion and distance from people created by large walled convents in the better parts of towns was felt to be negative and the living situation of religious women became a major question. She deliberately moved her Sisters' residence to insert themselves in the midst of people, particularly the poorer sections of society.

"Mother Teresa, before anybody else, recognised that the process of humanisation is an integral part of spiritual development. This recognition led to a revolution in the understanding of spirituality – from 'other-worldly' to 'this-worldly' – a genuine apostolic spirituality which recognised that Sisters work out their salvation by involvement in the human struggle for justice and peace.

"Apart from her philosophical contribution, her contribution was very tangible. She opened centres with a drop-in facility, where people with the HIV virus were made to feel welcome. She cared for people with AIDS and helped their families, partners and friends come to terms with the situation and the way it affected their lives. She saw her task as building bridges – bridges between hearts and bodies.

"She showed us that there is a universal sense of being challenged to live a much deeper Christian life with God at the centre and a recognition that to be a Christian today is to answer the call to be their best selves, to be fully human. Out of that she wanted to empower lay people to enable the kingdom to come and to journey with people through their lives. She instilled a very strong communal desire to be prophets and a sense of being called to reveal God in some way and a belief that if we fail to do so we fail the world.

"Mother Teresa was unequivocally taking the side of the downtrodden, the oppressed and the marginalised regardless of the personal cost or threat to her physical wellbeing. Can the same be said of us in Ireland today? Whose side are we on? What price are we willing to pay for championing unpopular causes or standing up for what we know to be right? While there is a remarkable generosity today towards organisations such as Trócaire and Concern are we, like Mother Teresa, willing to really put our comfort on the line? She challenges us to rediscover our prophetic role as Christians, a quality of life which attempts to give renewed heart to the Christian life by a radical commitment to simplicity, sharing and intimacy. She dares us to be double agents – people who observe the world as it is while in tandem imagining other worlds which might yet be. She reminds us in the sentiment of Karl Rahner that grace is in the air."

A Boatman for all Seasons

A soft-spoken, gentle man, Dick Warner was born in 1946 in England of Anglo-Irish parents. His grandfather was a Church of Ireland rector. As a child he travelled a lot because his father had itchy feet. The family lived, amongst other places, in Addis Ababa and Vienna and Dick got very little formal secondary education. Returning to Ireland in the early 1960s, he attended school briefly in Belfast and went to Trinity College Dublin. In the 1970s he joined RTÉ as a radio producer and later presented the four series of the internationally acclaimed award-winning *Waterways* television documentaries. Apart from his broadcasting work he writes books and articles and gives lectures on environmental topics. One of his most vivid memories of his radio programmes was of making a radio documentary on Mother Teresa.

"Jim Fahy and I went to Calcutta for five days to make the programme in the late 1970s. It was before she had won the Nobel Peace prize and she didn't have the profile then she has now. We lived in her convent and basically we followed her around on her daily routine beginning with Mass at 5 a.m. right through until 8 p.m. I'm not sure how long she maintained that same pace but at that time this frail, blue-eyed Albanian woman had incredible energy.

She had so many houses and places to visit: homes for the dying and destitute, a leper colony and so on. To my eyes she was a saint or almost a saint. It's pretty awe-inspiring not just to meet someone like that but to share her company for a reasonably lengthy period of time. Her conviction was absolute. I've never met anybody who allowed themselves less time for questioning. She had this wall of certainty about what her calling was. My enduring memory though is of her charity."

The trip to India had an unexpected sequel for him. He received a potentially devastating blow when he was diagnosed as having Multiple Sclerosis.

"MS cannot be diagnosed on one set of symptoms. I was having pins and needles and problems with my eyesight and went to my doctor. Having been in a leper colony when I went to India I read a book on leprosy and because of the similar symptoms I convinced myself that I had leprosy. When I told this to the doctor he nearly fell off his chair laughing! It's not possible to acquire the condition in the way I had envisaged."

The Life of Father Brian

Fr Brian D'Arcy is perhaps Ireland's best-known priest because of his extensive appearances in the media. He got the chance to know Mother Teresa:

"Mother Teresa is one person I'll never forget meeting. She had a look which was at once piercing and gentle. A look which said there is no sham in my life and there ought to be none in yours either.

"I interviewed her five or six times in all. Towards the end, age and work had taken their toll. She told me of an American benefactor who visited her in Calcutta. She was cleaning a leprous wound on a poor person's foot. 'I wouldn't do what you're doing for a million dollars,' he said. 'Neither would I,' answered Mother Teresa, 'But I do it for the love of Jesus.'

"She has spoken beautifully about the poor. Like the parables of Jesus, her experiences make the point effectively. She told me that the poor did not need our compassion or our pity; they needed our help. What they give to us is more than what we give to them. I think that is why her friend Pope John Paul II personally fast-tracked her beatification because '*She made those who had been defeated by life feel the tenderness of God*'.

"She challenged me to ask a lot of questions. Do we know our poor people? Do we know the poor in our house, in our family? Perhaps they are not hungry for a piece of bread. Perhaps our children, husband, wife are not hungry, or naked, or dispossessed, but are you sure there is no one who feels unwanted, deprived of affection? Where is your elderly father or mother?

"I have never forgotten the stories she told me: 'One day I visited a house where our Sisters shelter the aged. This is one of the nicest houses in England, filled with beautiful and precious things, yet there was not one smile on the faces of those people. All of them were looking towards the door. I asked the Sister in charge, 'Why are they like that?' The Sister answered: 'They are always waiting for someone to come to visit them. Loneliness eats them up, and day after day they do not stop looking. Nobody comes.' Abandonment is an awful poverty.

"On one of our nightly walks through London, I discovered a teenage boy, with long, well-groomed hair. He was sitting, thinking. I said to him, 'You shouldn't be here at this time. You should be with your parents. This is not a proper place for you to be at this time and on such a cold night.' He stared at me and said: 'My mother doesn't want me because I have long hair.' There was no other reason. A young man, a mere teenager, rejected by his own people, by his own mother. I reflected for an instant: maybe his mother is concerned about the hungry people in India, in Africa, or in the Third World. Maybe she desires to meet the needs of all except her son. She doesn't know that poverty, hunger, exists in her own house. It is she who provokes such hunger. That's why I ask: Do we know our poor people? Do we know how poor we ourselves are?

"In many places we have houses for the dying. I remember the day I picked up a woman in the street, thinking that she was starving to death. I offered her a dish of rice. She kept looking at it for a long while.

I tried to persuade her to eat. Then she said, with utter simplicity, 'I can't believe it's rice. I have been a long time without eating.' She condemned no one. She did not complain against the rich. She did not utter any bitter words. She simply couldn't believe it was rice.

"Yes, the poor are great. We have to love them, but not with pity. We have to love them because it is Jesus who hides under the likeness of the poor. They are our brothers and sisters. They belong to us. The lepers, the dying, the starving, the naked – all of them are Jesus.

"Her name was synonymous with 'doing good'. Even Diana, Princess of Wales regarded her a friend and a saint.

"In the last chat we had, in Knock, she told me that she had suffered from the crippling doubts for long periods of her life. She wondered if she was doing the right thing and found it hard to see where God was in the midst of so much poverty and suffering. That was a great comfort to me. Mother Teresa had doubts bordering on despair? It was at that moment that I saw her real sanctity, her true heroism. No journey is without crises."

The Singing Priest
Early in 1979, news broke that the Pope would visit Ireland that September.

The Pope's visit touched something very deep in the Irish psyche. It was like three Christmases rolled into one. Even the most sceptical were caught up in the occasion. Of course the fact that we got a day off from school was an added bonus. As we waited on Galway Racecourse on a misty September Sunday morning we laughed heartily at Fr Michael Cleary's warm-up performance of songs and jokes, a roller-coaster of fun and frolics.

As I munched my black-pudding sandwiches someone said: "Gawd, Cleary is a shockin' man. He's wasted in the Church. He should be on the stage. He'd make a fortune in Hollywood. Wouldn't he charm the venom out of a snake?"

After his death it emerged that he'd had a long relationship with his housekeeper and had fathered a son, Ross Hamilton.

I met Fr Mick for the last time in November 1993. In truth I didn't know him. I was shocked by the deterioration in his condition. Cancer and chemotherapy had ravaged the healthy-looking man I knew to an emaciated ghost of his former self.

He joked: "Everybody tells me I look better without the hair."

I lied through my teeth and agreed with this verdict.

As we parted he responded to the uncertainty and unreality in my voice as I wished him well: "I've a lot of fighting in me yet but if God calls I'm ready. Life is just a long courtship with God and death is the final union."

One of his final programmes on 98FM was about

Mother Teresa. He began by making a contrast between the values of the world and the values of Mother Teresa. He itemised the differences in the following way:

The World says:

Grab everything you can – take all you can get, wherever you can get it. Walk all over everyone who gets in your way and you will become rich and famous.

Mother Teresa says:

"Blessed are the poor in spirit. The Kingdom of Heaven is theirs."

The World says:

Only the strong survive. You must give ground to no one – you must allow no one to interfere with your plans, whatever the cost to anyone else – you must get everything you are entitled to and more.

Mother Teresa says:

"Blessed are the gentle. They shall have the earth as their inheritance."

The World says:

Be ruthless, don't take any prisoners, crush those who are weak – don't show any mercy to anyone in trouble – they are weak and nothing but a burden to society and above all a burden to you.

Mother Teresa says:
  "Blessed are those who mourn: they shall be comforted."

The World says:
  Never show any mercy. Mercy is only for the weak. Why should you tolerate other people's failures and mistakes? Compassion is for wimps. Remember the Bible said: "An eye for an eye and a tooth for a tooth."

Mother Teresa says:
  "Blessed are the merciful. They shall have mercy shown them."

The World says:
  Achieve your objectives no matter what the cost. If you have to hurt someone in the process – don't worry about it. If you have to kill someone, they were probably better off dead anyway. Don't feel bad if you have to eliminate someone – you are helping to make the world a better place.

Mother Teresa says:
  "Blessed are the peacemakers."

The World says:

Whatever you do, look after yourself. Let other people solve their own problems. Don't waste your time worrying about injustice, pain or suffering. Leave that to someone else. If you get involved in helping others, you will be dragged into their mess. Leave other people's problems to social workers and you will have a much more comfortable life.

Mother Teresa says:

"Blessed are those who are persecuted helping others. The Kingdom of Heaven is theirs."

Michael Cleary claimed that Mother Teresa through her work and life showed that God is a living God, someone who loves people and loves to be loved by people. He believed that she was the living proof of the old Celtic prayer that God is to be found with people not in places of stone:

Pilgrim, take care your journey's not in vain
A hazard without profit, without gain,
The King you seek you'll find in Rome, 'tis true,
But only if He travels on the way with you.

Fr Mick reminded his radio audience that the Irish description of a disabled person as God's own person (*duine le Dia*) is a good illustration of Mother Teresa's example that old life, injured life, disabled life, every life is God's own life, God's special gift and task.

Someone had sent him on the motto of the Sue Ryder Foundation and he quoted it with feeling – claiming that it could have been Mother Teresa's anthem:

For the cause that lacks assistance,
For the wrong that needs resistance,
For the future in the distance,
And the good that I can do.

"Her sentences provide an invaluable insight into her mind and character. She seems to have difficulty constructing a sentence without reference to God or one of the Holy Family. Listening to her speak one senses the struggle of someone trying to come to terms with their own limitations. Despite her strong faith, she is not cocooned from the reality of the world around her. Although thoughts of Godliness are as natural to her as breathing is to the rest of us, she has not been seduced into ignoring the problems which people have today. In fact she nurtures a deep desire to see a more loving and just society created."

And at the Hour of Her Death

Throughout much of the 1980s and of the 1990s Mother Teresa experienced health problems, many of them serious. Yet she continued to work away and travel frequently even when it would have been wiser not to. After a period of illness she died on Friday 5 September 1997. An Irish Franciscan priest Gearóid O'Connaire, who is based in Rome and at the forefront of a joint campaign run by the religious orders to achieve Justice, Peace and the Integrity of Creation had something of the inside track on the news:

"My doctor is Vincenzo Bilotta. He was Mother Teresa's doctor when she was in Rome and in her later years she had many health scares, especially with her heart. Dr Bilotta has a big photo of Mother Teresa in his surgery. After she died the Sisters in Calcutta rang him to tell him the news personally. He said that her heart, which had held up for all those years, just gave away."

Mother Teresa's death, at the age of 87, saddened the world. The Indian government gave her a state funeral, where the country observed a national day of mourning. Her last action was to lift her hand and touch and kiss the crucifix. Her final words were to offer her sufferings along with those of Jesus, all the while whispering, "Jesus, I love you. Jesus, I offer myself to you. My God, I thank you, praise you and adore you. Jesus, I love you . . ."

Her death was marked in Ireland in many ways. Mother Teresa's connection with Ireland was emphasised when Cardinal Seán Brady celebrated a

Mass for her in Saint Patrick's Cathedral in Armagh on September 10th 1997. In his address he said:

"On this day fifty-one years ago, September 10th 1946, Mother Teresa was travelling by train north from Calcutta to Darjeeling, in the foothills of the Himalays. Suddenly she had the inspiration to found a new order and devote herself to the poor. Last year, fifty years later, Mother Teresa came to Armagh to open the 563rd house of that new order – The Missionaries of Charity. She came here to this cathedral to pray in thanksgiving. At the end of the prayers, helped by two of her Sisters, the tiny frail eighty-five-year-old lady struggled to her feet. I said struggled because as a result of an accident she had sprained her ankle and was in a wheelchair. She spoke to us then about prayer and love, two topics which were close to her heart.

"I suspect that if she were here tonight she might return to those same subjects. She certainly would not wish this sermon to be a eulogy for herself. In 1971, when Malcolm Muggeridge wrote *Something Beautiful for God*, Mother Teresa asked that it should not be a biography of herself. 'The work is God's work,' she would say. Mother Teresa has died after an extraordinary life. Very many people feel a great sorrow and a great sense of loss at this time. For the abandoned and the outcasts, the little ones and the forgotten ones, she was a great sign of hope. They have lost a faithful and wholehearted friend.

"The greatness of Mother Teresa came from her close union with Jesus Christ. That union was nourished and strengthened by hours of prayer every single day of her life. Every morning you would find her in her convent at prayer before 5 a.m. There she knelt for hours on the ground without seat or kneeler, deeply absorbed in conversation with Jesus. I last saw her on July 1st. She was not well enough to come to chapel, so Holy Communion had to be brought to her in the infirmary. There she was with her bible and prayer book, in deep recollection, preparing for the coming of her Lord and Master.

"Some of you may remember that in Armagh that evening her Sisters gave out little prayer cards. 'Mother's business cards,' they called them. Mother Teresa wrote that prayer out of her own experience. Silence, prayer, love, faith, service, peace, sum up her whole life. It is in the silence of the heart that God speaks. We need to listen to God. It is not what we say but what God says to us in prayer and through us that matters.

"Mother Teresa is associated with feeding the hungry. *'I was hungry and you gave me to eat'* was one of her favourite scripture passages. She knew that there are different kinds of hunger in different parts of the world. There is the emotional hunger of those who are starved of love and affection. There is the spiritual hunger of those who had famished for want of purpose and meaning in life. She wanted to tackle those hungers as well. So she opened a house for contemplative Sisters in New York. Their vocation is to pray most of the day. 'Prayer feeds the soul,' she said. 'As blood is to the body, prayer is to the soul. Prayer brings you closer to God.'

"In the life of the Missionaries of Charity, more importance is given to prayer than to the actual work, but their work flows from their prayer life. Prayer puts people in touch with God and makes them capable of being His instrument. Prayer teaches us to look contemplatively at the world and to see there the living presence of Jesus. The Missionaries of Charity begin their day with prayer, both personal and communal, followed by the Eucharist, which is the real centre of their existence. Each evening they have an hour of adoration. The Sisters have a rule of reciting the rosary when travelling or while walking through the streets. Everything is done in an atmosphere of prayer.

"The source and strength of Mother Teresa's whole life was the twofold commandment of love of God and of neighbour. These two commandments cannot be separated. The fruit of faith is love. The Missionaries of Charity base their whole life on these two pillars, love of God and love of neighbour. They take a vow of wholehearted free service to the poorest of the poor. Every morning they recite this prayer: 'Make us worthy, Lord, to serve our fellow-men throughout this world who live and die in poverty and hunger. Give them, through our hands this day, their daily bread and by our understanding love give peace and joy.'

"What is the legacy of Mother Teresa? The question has been asked often in recent days. She has left us the wonderful example of her life. It was a life so filled with the love of God that she was totally devoted to helping those in pain, those in greatest need, those who live in the slums, those who die in the streets. This love is not patronising, for charity is not about pity. It is about love. So many people admired Mother Teresa because she lived a Christianity they could accept and identify with. She inspired so many people to imitate her and has challenged them to rise to tremendous heights of generosity and self-giving. 'Give till it hurts,' she said.

"Mother Teresa is a prophet for our times and of course like all prophets she is sometimes misunderstood. She speaks a language that a lot of people don't understand today, the language of humility and mercy for example, which is not so popular in a world which sometimes prides itself on being abrasive and assertive. She stands for reverence and respect. Respect for the weak as well as for the strong. Respect for all of God's children, regardless of who they are. She teaches us to be patient with the patience of God Himself who walks our roads with human footsteps.

"Mother Teresa was a great symbol of hope because she brought love and help to those who were shunned and abandoned. She was a real missionary of charity, someone sent to tell us of God's unconditional love for each one of us. She knew well that this love was revealed by Jesus Christ. It continues to be revealed by those who listen to his words: *'As long as you did it to one of these, the least of my brethren, you did it to me.'* Mother Teresa reminds us of God and of God's claims on our love and our time.

"Last week death took two remarkable women, Diana, Princess of Wales and Mother Teresa. They had met in life and become friends. Now they are joined in death. This evening we pray that they be united in the happiness of Heaven. There is a sign on the door of the house for the dying in Calcutta. It reads: *'I am on my way to Heaven.'* An older lady once said to Mother Teresa, 'I am full of fear. I am afraid of death. You can help me for you have seen many people dying.' Mother spent time with that fearful lady and talked happily about death. She explained her vision of death as going home to an always loving Father. The woman thanked her for comforting her by removing some of her fear. One of the great crosses in Mother Teresa's life was the fact that due to the situation in Albania she was unable to see her own mother for many years before her death. 'We will meet in Heaven,' she would say. We believe that those who enter into a relationship of friendship with Jesus and love one another, here on earth, already possess eternal life and that Heaven is the fullness of that life.

"May our prayer this evening deepen our own faith in the reality of life after death. May our reflection on the lives of those who have gone before us, prepare us for our own death. May it inspire us to see and to serve Jesus and the least fortunate. The fruit of service is peace. May our loving service help those for whom we have prayed to enter into the fullness of everlasting life, Amen."

Mother Teresa's death was a shared experience because of the television-created global village. Within minutes our television sets brought the sad reality into our homes with disturbing immediacy. The television images ensured that the event belonged to everyone. The mourning too, like that for Princess Diana, was a communal experience. Her followers united to grieve but in a safe and private place, even amid millions of other viewers, to grapple with the sadness that enveloped them. Yet even in their darkest moments those who felt they knew her clung to the comfort blanket of knowing that they were not alone in feeling disconsolate, sombre and sad.

The inscription on Mother Teresa's tomb reads simply:

"As I have loved you, you too love one another."

Following Mother Teresa's death the Holy See began the process of beatification, the first step towards possible canonisation, or sainthood. This process involves the documentation of a miracle. In

2002, the Vatican recognised as a miracle the healing of the tumour in the abdomen of an Indian woman, Monica Besra, following the application of Mother Teresa's picture. Mrs Besra claimed that a beam of light emanated from the picture, curing the cancerous tumour.

Mother Teresa was formally beatified by Pope John Paul II on October 19, 2003 with the title Blessed Teresa of Calcutta.

A second miracle is needed for her canonisation.

A Lesson in Human Compassion

Sr Stanislaus Kennedy has long been a prophetic voice against injustice in Ireland. She is the founder of Focus Ireland. As one of Ireland's best-known champions of the poor I thought she would be the best person to ask for a perspective on Mother Teresa's legacy:

"When she died she left behind two saris and a bucket, the sum total of her worldly possessions. Somebody once said to me that her secret was that she was free from everything and that meant God could use her. This tiny Albanian nun, winner of the Nobel Peace Prize, with her hands joined in the Indian gesture of greeting, taught the world the meaning of compassion. That was her great legacy to us, for the world needs to be taught compassion today more than ever before.

"Her name will be forever associated with the city of Calcutta, as Calcutta will forever be associated with her. Godfrey Moorehouse described Calcutta as 'the easiest place in the world to come close to despair'. He wrote: 'Every statistic that you tear out of the place reeks of doom. Every half mile can produce something that is guaranteed to turn the newcomer's stomach with fear and disgust or a sense of hopelessness.' People who have visited India often say they could never go back because they couldn't face the destitution and the misery. That was not Mother Teresa's response. Instead of turning away in despair, she was driven by her experience of the misery around to devote her life to the service of the poorest of the poor.

"We do not all live in Calcutta, nor do we all experience the sort of daily destitution that Mother Teresa devoted her life to alleviating. But Mother Teresa's lesson in human compassion isn't confined to Calcutta or other places where human misery is at its most acute. The world desperately needs to be taught that compassion is needed everywhere, in our own society, in our own communities. We have all marginalised and rejected people.

"Mother Teresa did not preach compassion, she lived it. She made personal intimate contact in her daily life with the rejected ones, the homeless, prisoners, the sick, the dying, the old, the lonely. Not only did she devote her life to marginalised people, but she inspired others to follow her and most important, by her love and attention to them, she rendered the invisible people of the world visible, she brought the most brutalised, rejected and marginalised people of the world to the centre of the stage. She taught us not only that the rejected ones of society need our love and our help, but that they have a vital role to play in calling the world to justice.

"Mother Teresa was revered as a great saint in her lifetime, but she was also criticised. People felt that she was too simplistic, too naïve, that she didn't do enough to challenge the structures in society that created poverty. That she didn't really understand, but Mother Teresa in herself and in her selfless commitment challenged the status quo.

"When I met Mother Teresa in Detroit in 1989, I knew immediately that I was in the presence of God. She was a woman of extraordinary simplicity, or utter sincerity and humility and of an indefatigable commitment to the marginalised.

"She was a woman of extraordinary faith, and prayer played a central role in her life. Clearly she drew her strength and inspiration from her relationship with God. Today, our ears can be dulled to the word of God. We live in an age of science and scepticism. And yet people are looking for people like Mother Teresa, people who are symbols of love and compassion, people who have a practical Christian faith.

"Mother Teresa's life challenges us to ask fundamental questions about death and our fear of death. We can hide from these questions, pretend that we are strong by putting up barriers around our vulnerability, our fragility and our weakness. But deep down we know that these questions are the only questions.

"But we cannot live our lives through figures such as Mother Teresa. We can learn from her, but we must then do our own bit. We must care for those around us who are in distress, in poverty, close to death, homeless; the care we show is alight in a dark and darkening world. As each of us plays our part, all the same lights, each one lit by one of us, form a pattern of light, glowing into the darkness; it is a powerful source of courage and challenge to the world."

The Final Farewell

Visual symbols and symbolic actions have a mysterious power and they reverberate in the memory: tearful, joyful citizens dismantling the Berlin wall block by block; a student standing defiantly in front of an advancing tank in Tiananmen Square; the red ribbons of AIDS concern, and the white ribbons of peace worn in Ireland during the last IRA ceasefire; the broad smile on the face of Aung San Suu Kyi in 1996 as she emerged from six years of house arrest to meet the people of Burma with flowers in her hair; a million people in the streets of Spanish cities mourning the murder of a young politician by ETA.

Recent Irish history testifies to the power of symbols; witness the bowler hats and insignia of the loyalist Orange marchers. In many towns and villages in Northern Ireland the very stones of the street are painted in loyalist or nationalist colours. Huge murals, with their massive images of the "armed struggle", lour over the street corners in towns on both sides of the sectarian divide. Most of the predominant symbols in Northern Ireland are sectarian: they stress difference, separateness, hostility, violence and above all they demonise the "other side".

Symbols define the community and its understanding of itself, its identity. Symbols give us our identity, self-image, our way of explaining ourselves to ourselves and to others. Symbols determine the kind of history we tell and retell.

As Mother Teresa's coffin was being taken to its final resting place a man quietly held the Irish tricolour as a tribute to her on the streets of Calcutta. No symbol speaks more eloquently of the deep bond between Mother Teresa and Ireland.

A Global Event

One of Ireland's best-loved television personalities, Mary Kennedy, offers a unique eyewitness testimony to Mother Teresa's funeral Mass, which included Archbishop Seán Brady as one of the concelebrants:

"I have been lucky in my broadcasting work to

come across heroes. A real highlight was when I was sent to Calcutta to do the live TV commentary on the funeral of Mother Teresa. This was my first visit to this part of the world and the level of poverty and destitution in the city shocked me. The noises of clapped out, spluttering engines was relentless as the cars and buses packed the streets and there wasn't an inch of pavement on view because of the absolute sea of people, some walking, some begging, some just lying down on the path asleep. I found myself literally stepping over sleeping men and women as I walked along, all of them emaciated, all of them poor and hungry. The whole experience was an assault on the senses and you'd have to be made of stone not to be moved by the plight of those gentle and beautiful people.

"I knew before going the high regard in which she was held but it wasn't until I was in Calcutta and witnessed the outpouring of love and grief first hand that I fully appreciated the effect this diminutive figure had on the lives of the poorest of the poor. I was amazed to see old and frail Hindu women kneeling on the streets, praying in front of cardboard boxes that they covered with satin and bedecked with incense sticks and little nightlights shining in front of pictures of Mother Teresa.

"I remember the altar set on a rostrum covered in the blue and white colours of Mother Teresa's Missionaries of Charity. All around the edges of the rostrum were pinned lotus blossoms. The scent of those flowers as we entered and right through the morning was uplifting and fragile; in keeping with the woman they were there to honour. The funeral began with the cortège leaving Saint Thomas's church in the compound of the Provincial House of the Loreto Order in Middleton Row. It passed through the streets of Calcutta which she walked for so many years taking in the sick and the dying. Everywhere the cortège passed was thronged with the people of Calcutta who were there to pay their final respects to this woman who made her home in their city and who they knew simply as Mother.

"Mother Teresa was eighty-seven when she died and in spite of her tiny frame she was a tower of strength to the poorest of the poor. As well as ministering to the physical needs of the people she cared for, she was aware that there were other problems besetting humankind. She was a world figure who spoke out on numerous occasions not only on behalf of the destitute and the dying but also to warn people in the more affluent parts of the world of the dangers of putting too much store by material wealth. She was greatly admired the world over and the list of the heads of state and other dignitaries who travelled to Calcutta for her funeral bears testimony to that. It was sad that one of her great admirers and champions, Princess Diana, had died so tragically a week before her. They had become friends and Mother Teresa paid tribute to Diana for being devoted to the poor. She said at the time of her death, 'All the Sisters and I are praying for her and all the members of her family to know God's speed and peace and comfort in this moment.' So many people around the world were plunged into grief by the untimely and tragic death of Diana and were grieving for a second time at the passing of Mother Teresa. Those heads of state who travelled to London for Diana's funeral found themselves together again a week later at the funeral Mass for Mother Teresa.

"I was fascinated to see so many women of note from around the world. Hilary Clinton was there, so was the Duchess of Kent, Queen Sofia of Spain, Sonia Ghandi from India, Queen Fabiola of Belgium, Madame Chirac wife of the French president, Queen Noor of Jordan, President Aquino of the Philippines. All of these influential women were gathered to pay their last respects to another powerful woman who devoted all her energies to the poorest of the world's poor.

"It was a privilege for me to be given the opportunity to be present at that funeral and to savour the atmosphere in the city and in the stadium during the Mass. There was a quiet in the hall, a calm, a peace and sadness at the passing of this great woman. Mother Teresa lay in repose in front of the altar; her mortal remains covered in one of her saris. You would be in no doubt as to the slightness of frame of this otherwise powerful woman because her feet were uncovered and they were tiny. Enormous wreaths of those highly scented lotus blossoms surrounded her. The Archbishop Henry D'Souza, the Archbishop of Calcutta, celebrated the Mass and her fellow Missionaries of Charity sang. It was a very moving and gentle occasion, dignified and unhurried.

"She taught a lesson of love always and felt that if you judge people, you have no time to love them. Although she realised the need for aid for the poor, her belief was that mere aid is not enough.

"There were mile-long queues, day and night, outside Saint Thomas's church while she lay in state. As the people of Calcutta filed past her remains, they prayed, cried, kissed her feet, lifted small children to touch her robes and left flowers by her side. There were banners, posters and billboards with messages of love for Mother Teresa all over the city. I remember one written in English in big bold black letters: *"We mourn for the loss of our Mother."*

"As I recall that day of Mother Teresa's funeral, I appreciate how special the whole experience was. In spite of the fact that Calcutta is polluted, overcrowded, extremely poor and very noisy, what I remember is the peace and calm and beauty of the people, and the love associated with Mother Teresa. It's nice to have the opportunity to recall that visit to Calcutta now that Mother Teresa has been beatified and to celebrate the message of love that she spread by the way she lived her life. That message of reaching out to others and remembering that every living soul on this earth is worthy of respect and care."

Mary's memories of Mother Teresa have become connected with her memories of her late mother, who died at Christmas 2001.

"To me, though, the great hero of my life was my late mother. She was so much part of my life that I miss her terribly. Mind you, there are also times when I feel her presence and those times are a great consolation. About a month after she died, I was driving home from somewhere and feeling very low and lonely and all of a sudden I felt this energy surge in my stomach, which took me totally by surprise. I didn't know where I was but I thought of her at that moment and then I felt it again. An almost breathtaking experience which I haven't had since but which I did associate with her presence at that time.

"The following Easter, I was trying to get my head around masses of information for work – a commentary that I'd been asked to do with about three days' notice. There I was at seven on the Sunday morning, transmission day, poring over the sheets of paper on the kitchen table and beginning to panic. I remember saying: 'Ma, I'm not on top of this. I need a dig out.' And within a couple of seconds, a shaft of sunlight came in through the kitchen door and spread at an angle right across the pages on the table. It was incredibly beautiful and then it was gone. Coincidence, perhaps, but a very happy and pleasant coincidence, during which I felt my mother's presence.

"At times, when I'm out running, particularly if I go very early in the morning, at around six o'clock, I am overwhelmed by a feeling of well-being, looking up into the trees and hearing the birdsong. It's at times like these that I feel my mother's presence around me.

"She was a kind woman. It was she who taught me the meaning of Mother Teresa's comment: 'Kind words can be short and easy to speak, but their echoes are truly endless.'"

The Poetic Presence

Mother Teresa has even indirectly contributed to Irish poetry. Talking to me about his poem "Hostel", the acclaimed poet Micheal O'Siadhail referred to her phrase "Something beautiful for God" which Malcolm Muggeridge famously used as the title of his biography of Mother Teresa.

Micheal introduced his poem for me:

"The founder of the L'Arche Communities, Jean Vanier, tells us: 'When the poor and weak are present, they prevent us from falling into the trap of power – even the power to good – of thinking that it is we who are the good ones.' It seems to me that at the heart of Mother Teresa's understanding was the realisation that her work was not an achievement but simply something done for its own sake, something beautiful for God."

Hostel

Station of ease for the broken or frail.
A tear in an ocean. And yet that welcome
At face value, a roof and warmth, a meal.
Vague signals of angledom.

So little. So short of grand revolution
We'll always want to dream of.
If only dreams could scoop or fill an ocean . . .
Thimbled gestures of love,

Some gift of falling for endless tasks
Berth this moment's care;
The scarred visage of a down-and-out who asks
If an ocean starts with a tear?

Patient logs of strays and have-nots.
A youth stubborn and hurt
Uproots and wanders. No one knows his
whereabouts,
Nomad and introvert.

Long headstrong years on the loose;
Now shattered and underfed
A quarrelsome body yields nightly to delicious
Mercies of bath and bed.

One evening and again he's gone
Without trace. No mendings. No rebirth.
Tiny alleviations, something beautiful done.
A caress on the face of the earth.

Something Beautiful for God

A heavy cloud of sadness came over me when I heard the news of the death of one of Ireland's greatest writers, John McGahern. Like many other people from the West of Ireland I had experienced his great generosity at first hand. I was reminded of one of his many astute observations to me that life is a riddle that only the dead can really answer. In his short stories the shadow of death is never too far away. It is no coincidence that McGahern began his life as a teacher. His writings can teach us so much about life and death in all their glories and contradictions.

To his last days John carried with him a burning memory of his own mother's death.

"People who took the time to offer support, guidance, understanding and acceptance during these early stages of grief are recalled with a special gratitude. I remember all who came to the house, and all who didn't come."

By coincidence I spoke to him shortly after Mother Teresa's death on a day so wet that even the puddles had waves on them. Unsolicited he told me what he thought about her. Typical of John, though, his response was very nuanced:

"I grew up in a very Catholic home. Catholicism cast a long shadow over all aspects of Irish society in the 1950s. There was a heavy wooden crucifix nailed up on a wall in most homes, flanked by pictures of sickly-yellow and gloomy apostles. More saints and wounded martyrs watched over other rooms. Reading material consisted largely of religious magazines like *The Sacred Heart*, *The Far East* and *The Messenger*.

"The great instrument of Catholic instruction was the catechism. Learning off catechism answers never constituted my idea of a good time – though like so many of my generation the questions and answers have remained enshrined in my brain:

"'Who must your first love be?'

"'God.'

"'And after God?'

"'Mary, my Mother in Heaven.'

"I recall that the Mission was greeted with some excitement in our parish. It became a distant second to the weather as the most important topic of conversation. The priest tried to drum up some enthusiasm and spiritual fervour by describing it as 'an occasion of grace'. Not that grace was ever much in evidence on those days. Public enemy number one was sin. The preparation beforehand was a fastidious enterprise.

"The trappings and ceremonial of services were

more elaborate and formal than normal and all the component parts were done with enormous care for detail. Even the choir's attention to musical offerings of praise were better than usual, rising from the truly awful to the simply bad. That hardy perennial 'Soul of My Saviour' was used throughout the week with reckless abandon. It was like using one's best china to feed the visitors, the family of workmen, the children at a birthday party and the dogs and cats.

"Nevertheless, for most people the mission was really a social event. This sharing of gossip and humour helped to keep the community alive, but also revealed the heartache and quiet desperation which underlined so many lives in the parish.

"The sermons went on and on. Now and again a crying or crawling child gave a bit of diversion to the rustling and waiting congregation. For all his piety my father was sceptical about the real value of the 'Reds', the priests of the Redemptorist order who specialised in giving parish missions.

"'They only make the pious a bit more insufferable and the sinner more despairing. Those priests are only strolling players. There's nobody so right as the righteous. Trying to get people to change their life by ranting and raving is about as sensible as trying to cut turf with a razor blade. But sure they are the only entertainment we get in the chapel all year.'

"I could not understand why my father could be so blasé about the whole thing. I found all the haranguing of sin and vice by the Hell-fire merchants very disconcerting. The talk was a blend of threat and fear. Those terrifying sermons lingered maddeningly with me. Little wonder I entered the confessional box trembling.

"I found this anti-sin campaign very confusing and very different from the pieces of the Gospel we read at school. The Jesus of the scriptures was a loving and merciful man, the milk of human kindness especially to those on the margins, a Saviour who came to call not the just but the sinners. Accusation and reprisal were the twin characteristics of the God of the preachers, not a compassionate healer but a grim reaper. Their God purified through terror.

"The locals had a competition about the quality of the preaching. Somebody who really excelled earned the distinction: 'He'd make the hair stand on your head.' A truly remarkable sermon merited the ultimate accolade: 'He'd make the hair stand on your head even if you were bald!' By contrast someone who was more intellectual and spoke in abstractions was dismissed in savage terms: 'He was so wishy-washy he was worse than watery tea.'

"Our school catechism seemed to owe more to the preachers in the Bible. We learned it by heart because we were led to believe its every word was the definitive truth. Everything was black and white. There were no grey areas. The only area for discussion was whether a particular sin was mortal or venial. The rule of thumb we learned was: 'When in doubt assume it's a mortal sin.'

"I think this emphasis on sin and fear was the main reason why I left the Church in my adult years. Yet I never forgot that there was beauty in Catholicism. I had, for instance a particular reverence for Benediction. I loved the choir's singing, the air warm and heavy with incense and bodies and the tinkling of a bell. There always seemed to be a chorus of shrouded coughing coming from the pews from nervous parishioners, answering awkwardly to the priest's promptings. In silence and solemnity the priest climbed towards the tabernacle. The monstrance glittering like a metallic sun as it moved it in the shape of a cross before a mass of adoring eyes. I marvelled at the altar boys, in scarlet and white as they left the altar in twos, in front of the priest bearing the empty monstrance, the light from the candles dancing daringly on the gold of his cloak.

"Mother Teresa's great value for Catholics and non-believers alike was to remind us that religion can be and should be a thing of beauty, illuminated by inexhaustible reserves of mercy and mission – a faith that inspires. I liked the way she popularised the phrase 'doing something beautiful for God'.

"I would have disagreed profoundly with Mother Teresa in a number of areas. However, I would have to concede that more than any other person I can think of she made us particularly conscious of the wisdom of Brendan Kennelly's incisive words, 'Self knows that self is not enough.'

"Ezra Pound's quotation is to me a brilliant summary of the Christian life: 'Nothing matters but the quality of the affection – in the end – that has carved the trace in the mind.'

"The force of love, of unexpected and invigorating vitality, rather than some judgmental doctrine is what ought to animate Christians and all good people. Only true love carries memorial weight, regenerates moments of tenderness, of unions of spirit. Such a love is never encountered in stony walls or architectural masterpieces rising to an impassive sky. Mother Teresa showed us that the primary obligation is not to build memorials to the dead but to give food to the living. She will always be a reminder that the secret of life is that only in love for the living is the spirit praised forever."

Chapter 7

Keepers of the Flame

Even after she left the Loreto Order, Ireland was never far from Mother Teresa's thoughts. Not surprisingly she was keen to establish a significant presence in the country she loved so well. She smiled when I mused that, with all the need in India, she felt compelled to send some of her Sisters here to Ireland. She replied in a soft voice: "To serve. If one gives a little bit of rice to a poor person in India, the person feels satisfied and happy. The poor in Ireland and the West do not accept their poverty, and for many it is a source of despair. We can be a bridge between those who have and those who have less."

In addition to the fact that a significant number of her Sisters are Irish, the most tangible evidence of Mother Teresa's connection with Ireland today is found in the work of her Sisters in Dublin, Sligo,

Armagh and Blarney, County Cork. In her life Mother Teresa's main flashpoint was not the number of problems, nor the scale of the problems but our collective failure to do anything to solve them. When action is called too often we respond simply with platitudes. When confronted with problems we simply wash our hands à la Pontius Pilate. Her frustration was not with our actions, but with our non-actions, by our collective sins of omission. She pointed out that if we were not part of the solution we were part of the problem. She believed that we are too inclined to put the difficult thing on the long finger. Instead we should do it as soon as possible because there is instant relief.

In the Ireland of today there are three possible responses for her Sisters to follow. They might be prophets announcing the better age to come. Alternatively they could be preservers, making sure that in the flux of life the validity of past insights will not be lost. However, Mother Teresa chose a third approach for them: to share the drama of the age and work for the advancement of society and the common good.

Dublin Can be Heaven

As I spoke to Mother Teresa in her Sisters' house in Dublin I asked her why specifically she had decided to open a house in Ireland's capital city. She paused for reflection before answering indirectly. She began by explaining why, unusually, her Sisters take four rather than the customary three vows.

"The vow of obedience means that we have to do God's will in everything.

"The vow of poverty is very strict in our congregation. We do not accept anything, neither church maintenance, nor salary, nor anything for the work we do, all over the world. Every Missionary of Charity is the poorest of the poor. That is why we can do anything. Whatever is given to the poor is the same for us. We wear the kind of clothes they wear. But ours is a choice. We choose that way. To be able to understand the poor, we must know what is poverty. Otherwise we will speak another language. We won't be able to come close to that mother who is anxious for her child. We completely depend on providence. We are like the trees, the flowers. But we are more important to Him than the flowers or the grass. He takes care of them, He takes much greater care of us. That is the beautiful part of the congregation.

"We take the vow of chastity, our hearts entirely dedicated to Christ.

"Finally we take a unique fourth vow – that of giving wholehearted free service to the poor. We cannot work for the rich. A mother has no doubt when she serves her child. Because she loves. It changes everything in her life. The same thing for us.

If we are really in love with Christ, this doubt does not come. Maybe a longing comes to do better, but not doubt.

"Our Sisters must go out on the street. They must take the tram like our people, or walk to where they are going. That is why we must not start institutions and stay inside. We must not stay behind walls and have our people come to us.

"How can you truly know the poor unless you live like them? If they complain about the food, we can say that we eat the same. The more we have the less we can give. Poverty is a wonderful gift because it gives us freedom – it means we have fewer obstacles to God and can give ourselves more fully to people in Ireland."

Mother Teresa believed that true poverty was the absence of the awareness of Christ present in the world and in the human person:

"It is in the giving that we bring Christ to others; it is through going out to others that we open their hearts so that Christ may enter and be present to them."

As a result she presented a very clear philosophy to her Sisters:

"I pray that you will understand the words of Jesus, 'Love one another as I have loved you.' Ask yourself 'How has he loved me? Do I really love others in the same way?' Unless this love is among us, we can kill ourselves with work and it will only be work, not love. Work without love is slavery.

"Renunciation, temptations, struggles are what surround the soul that has opted for holiness. I wanted our Sisters to see Jesus in each one of them. I asked them to touch that Jesus tenderly and devotedly as they touched Jesus in the Holy Sacrament; and to serve that Jesus whole-heartedly and with all their ability.

"I believe the people of today do not think that the poor are like them as human beings. They look down on them. But if they had that deep respect for the dignity of poor people, it would be easy for them to come closer to them, and to see that they, too, are children of God, and that they have as much right to the things of life and of love and of service as anybody else. Everyone is in a rush, and on the way there are people falling down, who are not able to compete. These are the ones we want to love and serve and take care of here in Dublin."

Mother Teresa was looking for a particular type of young woman to come and minister in Dublin and elsewhere in Ireland:

"Many make great sacrifices to come here, to share in the work of loving the poor, feeling the closeness of Jesus. Being here, for some, gives them the chance to really deepen their personal love for Him. There are so many beautiful Irish people who give so generously also.

"These girls wanted to give their best, because in our society we have to make a total surrender to God; this is the spirit of the community. They wanted to achieve this fulfilment in their own lives by giving all to God, giving up their position, their home, their future and dedicating all of it wholly to the poorest of the poor. They thought they couldn't give enough to God who had given this beautiful vocation of serving the poorest of the poor.

"One of our novices had just entered the congregation, after finishing her studies at the university. Before she and another Sister left to care for the poor one day, I reminded them, 'You know where you have to go. During the Mass notice how tenderly and lovingly the priest touches the Body of Christ. Do not forget, that Christ is the same Christ you touch in the poor.' The two Sisters left. One of them, the novice, knocked on my door. She told me, full of joy, 'Mother, I touched the Body of Christ for the last three hours.' Her face reflected her deep joy. 'What did you do?' I asked her. 'Right after we arrived,' she answered, 'they brought us a man covered with wounds. He had been picked up from the rubble. I had to help take care of his wounds. It took three hours. Therefore I touched the Body of Christ for three hours. I am sure it was him.'

"Side by side with their spiritual training, they have to go to the slums. Slum work and this meeting with the people is part of their training so that we all give our wholehearted free service to the poorest of the poor – to Christ in his distressing disguise. Because of this it is necessary that they come face to face with the reality, so as to be able to understand what their life is going to be, when they will have taken their vows and when they will have to meet Christ twenty-four hours a day in the poorest of the poor of the slums or in the streets of Dublin.

"When our Sisters come to Ireland they do so in a spirit of sacrifice. Once a group of teachers from the United States came to visit me in Calcutta. Before they left, one of them asked me if I would say something that they could keep as a remembrance of the visit and that would also be useful to them.

"I answered: 'Smile at one another. Smile at your wives.'

"One of them said, 'Mother, it is obvious that you are not married!'

"'Yes I am,' I answered. 'Sometimes it is very difficult for me to smile at Jesus because he asks too much of me.'

"Even when it is difficult for them our Sisters come to Ireland with a smile.

"Gandhi said he was impressed by 'your Christ but not your Christians'. If people in Ireland, like so many other countries, were as good at living Christianity as they were at talking about it there would be no need for our work here.

"It was St Vincent de Paul who used to say to

those who wanted to join his congregation: 'Never forget, my children, that the poor are our masters. That is why we should love them and serve them, with utter respect, and do what they bid us.' We treat the poor like they are a garbage bag in which we throw everything we have no other use for. Food we do not like or that is going bad – we throw it there. This does not show any respect for the dignity of the poor; this is not to consider them our masters, like St Vincent de Paul taught his religious, but to consider them less than our equals. That message still needs to be learned in Ireland today as well.

"One of my Sisters once read a passage to me:

Go with the people
Live with them
Learn from them
Love them
Start with what they know
Build with what they have
But with the best leaders
When the work is done
The task accomplished
The people will say
"We have done this ourselves."

"I hope our Sisters in Dublin and in Ireland will serve the people in that spirit."

From their base in South Circular Road the Sisters provide a range of services to people such as a food centre for homeless people and others in need, a home for mothers and children, free clothing and washing facilities and also short-term emergency accommodation, treating all they need in a holistic way.

Peter McVerry is a Jesuit priest. For years he has championed the cause of the marginalised in Irish society. He is particularly associated with the campaign to provide accommodation for homeless boys in Dublin. He keenly welcomed these Sisters to Ireland both for the work they do for people in need but also as a reminder of the spirit of Mother Teresa:

"We can never understand God. Our human concepts are too inadequate to capture the essence of who God is. But we can get glimpses of who God is, moments of illumination, which point us in the direction of God. The concept of compassion is one of those glimpses.

"Mother Teresa and compassion belong in the same sentence. She was universally admired for that compassion because people, I think, recognised that her life of compassion was the fulfillment of what it means to be a human being. Most of us are incapable of living that life of compassion, and so she reminds us of what we would like to have been.

"Mother Teresa also challenged the culture of our time: she looked on someone who had achieved nothing, who possessed nothing, who was in the eyes of many worth nothing, and she recognised that person's infinite value as a child of God.

"Mother Teresa was, like all of us, a person of her time. Her following of Jesus led her to bind up the wounds of each person she encountered at the side of the road. The command to 'love one another' was directed at those individuals who crossed her path. The compassion that impels us to challenge those political, economic and social structures, which were the causes of so much of the suffering of those she rescued, is a concept which arrived late in the life of Mother Teresa. The concept of structural sin, which recognises our participation in, and responsibility for, those structures, came even later. Mother Teresa's status and credibility could have made her an outstanding advocate for social and political change on behalf of the poor. But it is, perhaps, unfair to expect her to have embraced such concepts at an age her mindset had become less malleable. Certainly those of us who have only stood on the sidelines and admired her from afar are in no position to cast the first stone.

"Mother Teresa was one of those very few people who were canonised by popular acclaim, even before her death. For many people, she revealed the face of God."

A Day in September

Today five Sisters of the Missionaries of Charity are based in Armagh. Part of their role is to try to build bridges between the two communities. Rather than remaining a prisoner of history they seek in a very quiet way to help shape a new future in Northern Ireland where the traditional enmities are redundant. One of their biggest admirers is their near neighbour, Cardinal Seán Brady:

"I always consider that it was a great privilege for me to have met Mother Teresa – now Blessed Teresa of Calcutta. During my years in Rome I used to celebrate Mass once a week in one of the convents of the Missionaries of Charity. I also used to hear the confessions of the Sisters and give a short talk and impart Benediction of the Blessed Sacrament. Mother Teresa was present on a couple of occasions and she used to come to speak to me to thank me for what I was doing for the Sisters.

"I suppose the first thing that I noticed was that Mother Teresa was hardly noticeable at all. She knelt at the back of the group – bent low. On one occasion I gave Benediction and did not in fact advert to her presence. It was a very hot day in August. I suggested to the Sister in the sacristy that since they had already prayed the Holy Hour, we might consider omitting the talk. She exited the sacristy and was back within minutes to say, 'But Mother says you should say something.' I gathered my thoughts as quickly as I could, uttered a quick prayer to the Holy Spirit and did my best. I am sure that Mother Teresa was not really impressed but my vanity was consoled on another occasion when she asked for the text of my talk and I actually did have a text.

"I met Mother Teresa at Leonardo da Vinci Airport, Rome, and I was struck by the fact that she travelled light, very light indeed. When I asked for prayers for my family she agreed. Then she suggested that I consider promoting the idea of a vocation to a religious life and specifically to the Missionaries of Charity in my family circle.

"On a number of occasions I heard her address the newly professed Missionaries of Charity on the day of their profession. I got the impression of a lady who was totally absorbed by the presence and power of God in her life and in the people she met.

"I attended Mother Teresa's funeral in Calcutta. It was most edifying to see the devotion of so many – especially once again the poor – to a European Christian woman. All the usual barriers had been broken down in her case. I was delighted when she was declared Blessed Teresa of Calcutta. It is great joy and consolation to have met her, known her and spoken to her and to be able to count on the powerful help of her intercession in Heaven.

"I believe that I have learned most about Mother

Teresa from the many Missionaries of Charity whom I have met and known in their various convents in Rome and here in Armagh on Cathedral Road. They are truly amazing in their dedication to prayer, to the worship of God and in their service to the poorest of the poor. They are modern day 'Wise Women' who come to us generously from the East in search of Jesus and bringing with them, the gold of their love, the incense of their prayers and adoration and myrrh of their patient and healing care of the most needy."

Sligo Sisterhood

Perhaps Mother Teresa's most enduring legacy is her humanity. One of the most striking things about talking to her Sisters today is the recurring message that so many of them were attracted to the congregation because of the influence of the fact that their foundress was "human". That human quality is still very evident in the work of her Sisters in Sligo.

The contemplative branch of Mother Teresa's congregation in Sligo has four Sisters: Sr Claire Anne, Sr Maria Lina, Sr Marija Mira and Sr Emmanuel. Like so many Sisters their superior, American Sr Claire Anne, was and remains heavily influenced by Mother Teresa:

"I was born in Washington State and am a convert to Catholicism. I felt this strong call from God to become a nun but I had strong prejudices at the time against Catholicism. At the same time I had this strong urge to become a nun which refused to go away. Back then I knew nothing about religious life and was totally ignorant about how I should go about this. I had this long struggle within myself to finally say yes or no. Although I was conscious of the grace of God within me I was saying back to Him: 'Please don't make me wear black.'

"Then I read this book about this extraordinary nun in India and she was wearing white and a little blue. I wrote to Mother and told her my story. She wrote a very nice letter back to me but told me that I could not become a Sister in the Missionaries of Charity unless I was a Catholic. I sought advice from one or two others and one of the things that was said to me was that becoming a nun was not a good enough reason to convert to Catholicism. Yet I felt this pure call from God and with pure grace I got through what was a hard process of converting and in 1975 I joined the Missionaries of Charity.

"At the time we had only one house in the United States – now we have forty-five, or fifty-fifty if you include Canada. It was in the Bronx in New York. When I went to work there, with the high levels of crime and burning buildings it looked like a war zone. I never thought that America was like that. At the time in Europe we had only three houses in Rome and two houses in London. I began my training in London and then did my novitiate in Rome where I went on to make my final vows.

"I first met Mother Teresa in 1975. I felt a bit shy because I felt unworthy to be in her company. It was very special to meet someone so committed to God and the poor. She was so normal and reassuring. Mother had such a strong presence of God in her that every word she said you felt went straight to your heart. When she spoke to us as a group and tried to teach us I felt God was speaking directly in my heart and always felt moved to do what she said. She was charged with the presence of God.

"At every stage in my profession she received me. Part of the ceremony when I became a nun was for her to cut my hair. At the time I had lovely long hair and she snipped at it. I said: 'Mother, cut it all. I am so happy to give it and everything I have to Jesus.' She smiled at me because I think she was happy to see someone so willing to serve Jesus in love."

Mother Teresa's presence was a constant in Sr Claire Anne's life as her ministry unfolded:

"Every time I met Mother I had been struck by her twin emphasis on meeting Jesus in the Eucharist and in the poor.

"In 1984 I was sent to Africa. Mother told me herself. Actually I went with her at one stage to set up our first foundation in Zaire.

"In 1996 I joined the Contemplative Branch of the order which had been started in 1976.

"In 1997 I picked up the phone on a Friday evening at seven. It was our day of silence, solitude and fasting. One of our Sisters said to me down the line: 'Mother's gone home to God.' I let out a deep sigh. I put down the phone. Although I felt sorrow I was very peaceful. I didn't get hysterical and didn't cry. My attitude was that she had achieved her life's desire which was to be with God in heaven. I opened the door and told each of the Sisters in the house from the superior to our novices. I said: 'Mother's gone.' Each Sister took the news in different way but we all went to the chapel. There was a sense of great loss. It was only when I watched the television coverage of her funeral that I cried. To this day whenever I see footage of her funeral I feel a strong sense of grief. I still miss her. All the Sisters do. We are sad that we don't hear her voice and of course we miss her presence.

"I feel she lives on in me. We all try in the Missionaries of Charity to let her live on in each of us."

In May 2009 a new chapter of Sr Claire Anne's life began when she came to Ireland:

"I was sent to Sligo. I never asked to go on a mission. We are almost always sent unless in exceptional circumstances a Sister volunteers to go to a particular place. I see obedience as a great blessing. When I was in Africa I faced dangers and difficulties that I never remotely would have considered myself capable of confronting or coping with – but I did.

"When I heard about the foundation in Ireland I was interested in it so it came as a great joy to be sent to Sligo. The Irish people are so courteous, generous and hospitable.

"While Mother was so focused on the poor she was equally devoted to the Eucharist and she gave so much time to adoration of the Blessed Sacrament, prayer, contemplation and study. She believed in Saint Augustine's idea of 'mingling mercy with misery'. For a few days a week, then, we are involved in the apostolate and street ministry and the service of the poor. However, our priority is to spend time with Jesus.

"In our convent the Evening Prayer of the Church is celebrated from six until seven daily and it's open to the public to join us in prayer.

"The centenary year began for us last August within our family of the Missionaries of Charity. The public celebrations will start in August 2010. For us here in Sligo we will be marking the event with a big Mass in the Cathedral which will be celebrated by Bishop Jones. We are all looking for ways we can promote Mother's message. I have so many memories of Mother. Each time I met her brought me new awareness of her faith. Each meeting with her was a deep privilege and very special. I am very happy because I feel so loved by God and Jesus. That is the source of my happiness and I know that's what Mother would have wanted for me. Even now we are still getting to know her better. It is only since her death that we have access to her spiritual writings and we have discovered that for most of the time we knew her she lived in a spiritual darkness. St John's Gospel concludes with the lines: 'There was much else that Jesus did; if it were written down in detail, I do not suppose the world itself would hold all the books that would be written.' I really think you could say the same about Mother – particularly if you include the stories of all the people she came into contact with."

The importance to the order of the Sisters' role in Ireland in general and in Sligo in particular was reflected in July 2009 when the head of the order, Sister Mary Prema, visited the Sisters' convent in Sligo. Sister Mary had been a teacher of disabled children and met Mother Teresa in Berlin in 1980 and decided to enter the congregation. On her visit to Sligo she began by reflecting on her memories of Mother Teresa:

"I found her to be a person full of energy and joy, who met people and shared the love of Jesus with them. She made me feel welcome and accepted and shared the common life with the Sisters and always had time to listen to them."

She observed that the work of the Sligo

community was "especially spiritual and prayerful" and visitors were welcome to join the nuns in the adoration of the Blessed Sacrament every day: "Many also come to confide in the Sisters and to ask them for prayers, and in sharing many of them find strength to accept whatever cross they have and to put their trust in God's merciful love. The Sisters also spend two hours a day going out to meet people in their homes, hospitals and nursing homes, and especially in the street."

Finally she outlined the priorities for the congregation in Ireland in the years to come: "I hope we can continue to go out in search of the poorest of the poor and identify new poverties, especially that of people who do not know and love God. I would also ask that people pray for me that I may recognise the plans that God has and that I may embrace them."

One person who is intimately aware of the Sisters' work in Sligo is the local Bishop Christy Jones. Mother Teresa remains an inspiration to him:

"Mother Teresa came on a visit to our cathedral on Sunday the 17th June 1996. A great friend of mine, Detective Tom Staunton, now deceased, borrowed Peter Henry's Mercedes and we both went out to greet and meet Mother Teresa at Sligo Airport. As we arrived at the airport there were uniformed Gardaí everywhere. I wondered why so much security? Were they afraid she would be shot or kidnapped? Who would consider doing that to such a beautiful lady? It was only later that the penny dropped. Most of the Gardaí had come out in their uniforms simply to meet this great woman of our time.

"Mother Teresa had fallen before coming so she had to be taken around in a wheelchair. Again as photographs show, many Gardaí were all together organising a wheelchair. What a beautiful expression of faith and hope in a great lady."

Bishop Jones had strong personal impressions of Mother Teresa:

"Quite honestly from the moment I met Mother Teresa I felt I was in the company of someone very close to God. She was frail but transparently holy. Her visit was transmitted to every home on local television. Prior to her arrival there were too many warnings of traffic, gridlock etc. which succeeded in keeping too many at home watching her visit on local television. However, the cathedral was full and we had a lovely period of prayer, Benediction and blessing. Mother Teresa addressed the people in the cathedral and outside from a platform. She spoke at length on the dignity of the human person, the gift of life and love and of course on the right of the unborn to life.

"Mother Teresa, I think, would prefer us not to give help to the poor unless we first accept and treat them with love as children of God. She stressed the dignity of every human person made in God's image and redeemed in the Blood of Christ. She sees all of us on a journey from different directions to God. The closer we come to God on the journey, the closer we come to each other. Mother Teresa was also convinced that she herself and all missionary Sisters of Charity were called not to serve poor people but "the poorest of the poor for whom nobody cares, those whom nobody wants or loves".

"Mother Teresa had obviously a very loving relationship with Jesus like the love of a spouse for a bridegroom in marriage. She acknowledged that for men it was more difficult to share such an intimate love for Jesus. These are her own words: "We must cling to Jesus, like a married couple who leave everything and everybody in order to cling to each other. We are spouses of Christ. Of course for us women it is easier to understand when we say we are spouses of the crucified Christ. Be only for Jesus. Be holy."

Bishop Jones felt emboldened to make a request of the distinguished visitor from India:

"As we drove back to the airport with Mother Teresa and Sr Nirmala who succeeded her as the International Superior of the Missionaries of Charity, I asked if the congregation would be willing to open a convent in our diocese. Six months later Sr Nirmala wrote to say that Mother's prayers had been answered and a community of Missionary Sisters of Charity would be formed in the

Elphin diocese. Thank God, ever since we have a vibrant community of Missionary Sisters of Charity in our town of Sligo. They are a contemplative community and I am convinced that their contemplation brings blessings beyond measure on our diocese.

"The Church has determined that Mother Teresa is one of the blessed in heaven. Please God she will very soon be canonised as a saint. She is the first person I have known personally on this earth whom the Church now numbers among the blessed in heaven."

Blarney Blessings

In recent times Mother Teresa's Sisters have sought to respond to the changing realities by establishing new structures and small communities. This more intimate environment is a far cry from the pre-Vatican II days when nuns' rooms were called "cells". This requires a whole new participative style of leadership with all the Sisters involved taking more personal responsibility in all aspects of their life. These Sisters share a need to be in touch with reality and with the presence of God in their lives and in the people they serve. The congregation's tradition of service to those on the margins finds new expression in their house in Blarney.

The importance of the work of the Sisters in Blarney was recognised on Wednesday 29th October

2003 when the then Bishop of Cloyne, John Magee, celebrated a Mass of thanksgiving for the Beatification of Mother Teresa, in the Church of the Immaculate Conception in Blarney.

In his homily Bishop Magee said:

"*'Love does not come to an end.'* (I Cor. 13:8)

"Just ten days ago, as the autumn sun beamed down on the vast crowd in St Peter's Square in Rome at the end of the Beatification Ceremony of Mother Teresa of Calcutta, a journalist approached me and asked me to put in one sentence what the Beatification of Mother Teresa meant for me. I replied that for me it was the glorification of Love lived, at all costs, in keeping with the Heart of Jesus. Mother Teresa, through her living out in her life the commandment of love – *"to love as I have loved you"* – became Blessed Teresa of Calcutta because she identified herself with the Person of Jesus who she encountered every day in her prayer life, in the Eucharist and in the service of the poorest of the poor. Small in stature, frail in appearance, Mother Teresa was a colossus in our time.

"The story of Blessed Teresa of Calcutta's life will be told throughout the world and the wonders the Holy Spirit did through her life will continue to inspire generations to come. Her decision to leave the relative comfort and security of the Loreto convent in Calcutta for the hardship and insecurity of the slums of that enormous metropolis can only be explained by what she called her 'inspiration' . . . On that day, in a way she would never explain, Jesus's thirst for love and for souls took hold of her heart and the desire to satiate His thirst became the driving force of her life. Mother Teresa had a blind trust in the God who loved her and who called her. She began her mission with nothing. She identified with the poor in everything, with those whom the world seemed to reject and ignore, in her own words with 'the unwanted, the unloved, the uncared for'. If Mother Teresa was to work among the poor, with the poor, and for the poor, then she thought she better wear the dress of the poor. So she dressed herself in the simple white sari with a blue border, the dress worn by women working as scavengers in Calcutta. She would give this new religious habit a new symbol and meaning: for her the white sari came to represent holiness, and the blue border stood for our Holy Mother, Mary. Just as Bengal's women kept the keys of their houses well tied up on one end of their sari, so Mother Teresa tied a small crucifix to one end of her sari, the key to her home in heaven.

"Mother Teresa had an indomitable will. Once she decided, under the inspiration of the Holy Spirit, to do something beautiful for God among the poorest of the poor nothing would stop her. I personally experienced this determination when Mother came to

Rome to establish her first house among the poor of the Eternal City. Throughout her life, anything worth doing for the poor was worth doing, no matter what the cost. She was conscious of what she called her uselessness, her emptiness. She would say: 'Nothing is possible for me. Nothing. I am utterly useless, like a bottomless bucket. I am good for nothing.' She would turn to God who called her and say: 'My God, You, only You. I trust in Your call, in Your inspiration. You will not let me down. Lord, You are my strength, You alone. My being and all that I think to be mine belong to You. Use me to make me worthy of any use. Is it not You who turned me out of Loreto? Was I not of some use inside that convent? But now, be with me. I can't do anything without You. I can't see anything. I am groping in the darkness. Lord, lead me into the light. Lead me as you like.' Jesus would say to her: 'Come, be My light.'

"When her work among the poor and her total dedication to their welfare began to attract others to join her she needed a home from which to work, a home for Jesus, for His co-workers and for His special poor and so she turned to the Mother of Jesus with the same trust with which Mary had turned to her son at the Wedding Feast of Cana.

"Mother Teresa recited the prayer, 'The Memorare' many times and never gave up. She got what she needed at 54A Circular Road in Calcutta, which residence became the Mother House of her new congregation. Her practice of placing the Miraculous Medal in places where she wished to establish a convent and a home for the poor showed her trust in her heavenly Mother, under whose patronage, as the Immaculate Heart, she had placed her congregation. Indeed, I can testify personally to this foresight and trust of Mother Teresa. When I was ordained Bishop in Rome in 1987, she gave me a Miraculous Medal, and said: 'Bishop John, I want a home for my Sisters in your diocese.' She came here personally to Blarney to bless the opening of the Missionaries of Charity convent in 1996. By 1997, the year of her death, or should I say her birth into heaven, Mother Teresa's Sisters numbered nearly 4,000 members and were established in 610 foundations in 123 countries of the world. Is this not a miracle in our times for one who considered herself useless and a bottomless bucket?

"The whole of Mother Teresa's life and labour bore witness to the joy of loving, the greatness and dignity of every human person, the value of little things done faithfully and with love, and the surpassing world of friendship with God. But there was another heroic side of this great woman that was revealed only after her death. Hidden from all eyes, hidden even from those close to her, was her interior life, marked by an experience of a deep, painful, and abiding feeling of being separated from God, even rejected by Him, along with an ever increasing longing for His love. She called this inner experience 'the darkness'. The 'painful night' of her soul, which began around the time she started her work for the poor and continued to the end of her life – fifty years in all – led Mother Teresa to an even more profound union with God. Throughout the darkness she mystically participated in the thirst of Jesus for souls, in His painful and burning longing for love and she shared in the interior desolation of the poor. The Holy Father, in reference to this aspect of Mother's life said: 'In the darkest hours she clung even more tenaciously to prayer before the Blessed Sacrament. This harsh spiritual trial led her to identify herself more and more closely with those whom she served each day, feeling their pain, and at times, even their rejection. She was fond of repeating that the greatest poverty is to be unwanted, to have no one take care of you.'

"Today we address Mother as Blessed Teresa of Calcutta. Each year her Feastday will be celebrated on the 5th of September, the anniversary of her going from this world to the home prepared for her by God. This evening we gather together here in Blarney with her Sisters, the Missionaries of Charity, with those whom they serve, with their co-workers and friends, to thank God for the wonderful things He has done in her. In a very special way we thank

Blessed Teresa for having given to this Diocese of Cloyne and to the Parish of Blarney an abiding presence of her life's work in the persons of the Sisters, the Missionaries of Charity. We cherish you, Sisters, and all the co-workers who give of their best in the service of those in need, especially the poorest of the poor. You are indeed a blessing for our Diocese.

"In the words of the Holy Father spoken on the occasion of the Beatification Ceremony just ten days ago: 'Let us praise the Lord for this diminutive woman in love with God, a humble Gospel messenger and a tireless benefactor of humanity. In her we honour one of the most important figures of our time. Let us welcome her message and follow her example.' Mother Teresa has been declared by the Church Blessed in Heaven, so that we might invoke her intercession with the God she loved so intensely and learn from the example of her life. If she were here this evening, as she was in 1996, what would she say to you and to me? Her challenge is to remember that whether we give service or disservice to our brothers and sisters we always do it to Jesus. May we learn to serve and to love as Jesus taught Blessed Teresa, and may we see and love in everyone we meet the face of the Lord who thirsts for souls and longs for love. Finally, may Blessed Teresa of Calcutta intercede for her Sisters here in Blarney, bless the service of love they are rendering to those in their care, and give us all a deep respect of and loving care for all."

Where Do We Go From Here?

Mother Teresa had been a certainty in an uncertain world for the Missionaries of Charity. Such was the force of her personality it was always going to be a huge readjustment for her Sisters after she passed on. Memory is our way of holding on to those we love. The memory of magical moments with her lingers for life in her Sisters' minds and those who knew her, leaving a warm after-glow to light up numerous conversations years later. Mother's memory will always be inside of her Sisters and they know that wherever they go in life she will flare up in their minds and they will feel both her warmth and spirit. While the sense of loss from her death will always reverberate in their hearts they must find a way to live on while never forgetting.

In the third millennium the Spirit in all its diversity is drawing the Missionaries of God to uncharted waters in Ireland with all the excitement and uncertainty that such change brings. The fact that this spirit is blowing throughout the congregation is the most conclusive evidence that the congregation is still vibrant.

When Pope John XXIII was Cardinal in Venice,

one night he was sitting down for his supper and his secretary came in with the file of a priest who was in trouble. The assistant was very disdainful as he spoke about the priest who was having a bad time. John pointed at his glass on the table and asked his secretary who it belonged to. "You, your Eminence," replied the puzzled secretary. Then Pope John picked up the glass and threw it on the ground where it smashed into smithereens. "Now, who owns it now?"

"It's still yours, your Eminence."

"No matter what the man did, he is still my priest," said Pope John.

It was a very forceful statement about his care for the broken person. Many of the Irish people who come to the Missionaries of Charity are victims because of abuse, broken marriages, shattered relationships, economic hardships and mental health problems. Brokenness is the rule rather than the exception. Some are coming to terms with the fact that they have created a situation that is irrevocable; something that can never be the same again. Crippled by the circumstances and mistakes of their past they go through life with an air of hopelessness. For some the wound has healed but the scar remains.

A large number of people who come to them are lonely, and in need of companionship and love. The Sisters believe that the greatest gift they can give to another is the gift of their time: time to listen, time to care, time to make them feel worthwhile. Part of their inheritance from Mother Teresa is the conviction that they can do a lot of good without seeking any attention for it. Over ten years on from their founder's death, the challenge has not changed for these Sisters. How are they going to care for those who are thought of as the Least, the Last and the Lost?

In the Old Testament people looked forward to a God "who would not cherish anger but would delight in showing mercy". Graham Greene famously remarked in a *cri de coeur*: "You can't conceive of the appalling strangeness of the mercy of God." The Sisters believe that they need to be living witnesses to that mercy.

I asked Mother Teresa if she ever worried about the future of her congregation once she had passed on. She shook her head emphatically and said:

"God pays attention to our love. Not one of us is indispensable. God has the means to do all things and to do away with the work of the most capable human being. We can work until we drop. We can work excessively. If what we do is not connected to love, however, our work is useless in God's eyes. Just as God has found me, He will find somebody else. The work is God's work, and He will see to it."

Judging by the evidence of her Sisters in Ireland today, Mother Teresa's confidence seems fully justified.

They believe that loving Christ means loving Him in His living Church in the here and now. They are close to people, healing and nurturing, challenging oppressive systems and structures, reaching out to those who need help and hope, praying with people rather than for them.

They are the keepers of Mother Teresa's flame. So what advice had she for these Sisters in Ireland?

"God does not call the qualified to work with the poor – he merely qualifies the called. Do your best; let God do the rest. Make sure that whatever you do has God's fingerprints all over it."

Given that her working life was coming to an end I asked her if she looked back and wondered if she wished she had done more. She replied almost in a whisper: "God called me to be faithful, not successful."

Chapter 8

A Place in our Hearts

It would never have occurred to Mother Teresa to speak of a Missionaries of Charity spirituality. It would appear that like many institutes of the time she followed an eclectic spirituality, taking influences from a variety of sources. Some of these had a strong Irish connection, including John Henry Cardinal Newman. Although born in England, Newman has very strong Irish links. Initially he was an Anglican but he converted to Roman Catholicism. In the 1850s he came to Ireland at the invitation of Paul Cullen, Archbishop of Dublin, to be the rector of the Catholic University. He commissioned the University Church on St Stephen's Green. Although he failed in his objective of creating the intellectual headquarters for Catholics of the English-speaking world, he was a formative influence in the development of what we know today as University College Dublin. His writings continue to be influential to many and Mother Teresa was one of his many admirers:

"There is a prayer that the Missionaries of Charity pray every day. Cardinal Newman wrote it:

Jesus, help me to spread your fragrance wherever I am.
Fill my heart with your Spirit and your life.
Penetrate my being and take such hold of me that my life becomes a radiation of your own life.
Give me your light through me and remain in me in such a way that every soul I come into contact with can feel your presence in me.
May people not see me, but see you in me.
Remain in me, so that I shine with your light, and may others be illuminated by my light.
All light will come from you, Oh Jesus.
Not even the smallest ray of light will be mine.
You will illuminate others through me.
Place on my lips your greatest praise, illuminating others around me.
May I preach you with actions more than with words, with the example of my actions, with the visible light of the love that comes from you to my heart.

Amen."

Just as Mother Teresa was influenced by Cardinal Newman, she in turn would influence many people in Ireland and beyond. At the beginning of CS Lewis's Narnia books, the Beaver makes the point repeatedly that Aslan is not a tame lion. The lion has a challenging, even dark, side as well as a comforting one. In death as much as in life Mother Teresa continues to be a source of challenge and inspiration and an object of devotion to many Irish people. This chapter considers some of them as a representative cross-section.

A Mother's Love

Gertie Shields knows the secrets of pain. On May 17th 1974 she thought she had her brush with great tragedy when her aunt, Concepta Dempsey, was one of the thirty-three people killed in the Dublin Monaghan bombings. However, nine years later tragedy cast another long shadow over Gertie's life when her daughter Paula was killed by a drunk driver.

"On February 19th 1983 the world as it was then ended for our whole family. Paula had left home on that Friday night well and happy. She was a pretty, intelligent girl of nineteen. She and four of her friends were killed by a 'drunken driver' of an articulated truck. Her best friend Sheilagh, whose twentieth birthday it would have been two days after, died instantly. Laura Cogan, twenty-two, and Michael and Martin Bollard, aged eighteen and twenty-two, also died. Paula gave up her fight for life at 4 o'clock the following afternoon. Laura never regained consciousness. Paul Gilsenan, a sixth victim, died some weeks later.

"It was an awful shock and still today it's like a dream. You'd wonder did it happen or did you dream it or whatever. It was total devastation.

"The funeral and the weeks following were a time of unreality. I did not seem to realise that Paula's death was permanent. Slowly the real horror sank in. I cried so much that I fell asleep from exhaustion. Never again would she come home with a light step and say, 'Hi, Mam, I'm home'. When the cold bleak February morning came I did not want to face the day. It was agony to open my eyes. Why could I not die in my sleep and be with her? It was hard to distinguish dreams from reality. The pain in my heart was a physical thing.

"The sound of the train she normally came home on in the evening brought fresh agony. Everywhere I looked there were reminders of her. When I met her friends I could not help thinking: why has it to be Paula who met this selfish drunk, who had driven the cab of an articulated truck having consumed, 'at least ten pints' on his own admission?

"I suppose our anger was compounded by the way the case was dealt with in the courts. The driver got away virtually scot-free. Yet in the very next case a man was given a six months' prison sentence for stealing some sheep. Were a few sheep worth more than my beautiful daughter?"

Gertie's sorrowful mysteries have coloured her attitude to many things including her feelings about Mother Teresa: "She was a woman who understood about compassion and about reaching out to broken people. I found it consoling to think that as my daughter Paula watches down on all of us from Heaven she has Mother Teresa there somewhere close by if she ever needs any comfort. I am not sure if compassion is ever required in Heaven, but if it is Mother Teresa will be there to dish it out to all those like Paula and Concepta who were taken from us too soon. Mother Teresa made the world a better place. I have no doubt that at this moment she is making Heaven a better place too."

Gone but Never to be Forgotten

The late John O'Donohue came to international prominence with the publication of his book *Anam Cara: Spiritual Wisdom From the Celtic World* (Bantam Press, 1997). It became a publishing phenomenon and remained on the bestseller lists for two years. He was a philosopher and a poet and held a doctorate in philosophical theology from the University of Tubingen in Germany. He spoke with authority and gravity, and with an instinct for the most appropriate detail, with a scrupulous yet enhancing accuracy though he bore no trace of strain, no whiff of midnight oil, his knowledge was obviously the product of much loving labour.

When I talked to John shortly before he died he explained that in his view the significance of Mother Teresa to contemporary society was to overturn the contemporary perception of spirituality and argue that instead of seeking to satisfy our spiritual hunger on an everlasting journey of exploration, we should seek an understanding that the soul is the house of our belonging. It is ever-present and is ever-ready to dispense peace and wisdom to enhance our life experience. This presence is nurtured in silence.

"The mystery never left Mother Teresa alone. Behind her image, below her words, above her thoughts, the silence of another world waited. A world lived within her. When she loved the poor she opened her life to an Other and as the body is in the soul, when she let someone near, she let them become part of her very self. In the sacred kinship of her soul she longed to share this gift of love and friendship with others. Her body was the home of her soul on earth and through her senses she felt the presence of the divine. To be wholesome, she remained truthful to her vulnerable complexity. In order to keep her balance, she needed to hold the interior and exterior, visible and invisible, known and unknown, temporal and eternal, ancient and new, together. No one else could undertake this task for her. You are the one and only threshold of an inner world. She knew that in this complex world that if you sell your soul, you ultimately buy a life of misery. She had no fear of death, as it has been with her since birth and was only the completion of her life's cycle. By releasing herself from the earth of death, which is the root of all our fears, she freed herself to live her life more fully. Like the fourteenth-century mystic Meister Eckhart before her, she believed that outside God there is nothing but nothing.

"God chose to be definitively revealed in the human person Jesus of Nazareth which is a marvellous affirmation of the dignity of the human person. The Incarnation illustrates as nothing else and in no other way the full measure of human responsibility and human destiny. The unknown God who is lord of the universe discloses to people that if they want to know what God is like, they should look here – at a human life.

"On Good Friday Jesus reached into the depths of sorrow, when this God-man experienced the physical agony and the mental degradation that so many people experience today. It was as if he deliberately entered, imitated, the most painful dimensions of being human, plumbing it to its unspeakable depth. Yet Mother Teresa reminds us that God was present in our suffering, hanging on the cross of contradiction, and that life flows from this dark mystery.

"In Connemara the phrase used to describe popularity and admiration is '*Tá aghaigh an phobail ort*': the face of the people is towards you. This is particularly relevant in Irish society given the evils of sectarianism and the need for an ecumenical approach to the search for truth. The phrase ought to be a presence for reconciliation in a country that has been disfigured by violence and serves as a constant reminder that we must all intensify and improve still further our efforts for lasting peace. There was a rich ethical fragrance to Mother Teresa, reminding us of our responsibilities to other people. In a sense she was a prophet challenging us to create a society where, in the words of the Irish poet John Hewitt, '*each may grasp his neighbour's hand as friend*'.

"At her inaugural address Mary McAleese observed: 'We know our duty is to spread the benefits of our prosperity to those whose lives are still mired in poverty, unemployment, worry and despair. There can be no rest until the harsh gap between the comfortable and the struggling has been bridged.' One of the most positive contributions of Mother Teresa has been her emphasis on social justice. No one has done more to advance this theological evolution than her. She brought a welcome focus on the fact that the social dimension is not an optional extra but a constituent part of the Gospel in a fundamentally formative sense.

"To talk about her faith would be easy – a much more difficult task is to find words to express the sincerity which was evident in everything she said. Her world was amplified to the sound of compassion."

The Good Shepherd

Mike Ryan is an English teacher from Cork who has a deep devotion to Mother Teresa:

"I am fascinated by Christianity and the figure of Christ. I constantly marvel at the fact that those who are followers of Christianity believe that even before we were born and long after we die, there is at work a provident, gracious God who has created us and loves us and wants us to share in God's own life. This view shapes the Christian's moral life by enabling them to live in faith, in hope and in love. Accordingly, Christianity issues us with an invitation into the heart of what it is to be human. I love the idea of the divine being most tellingly revealed by our humanisation.

"Of course as someone who has spent a lifetime studying, in various ways, words, I particularly admire the statement in the Gospel: *'In the beginning was the Word, and the Word was with God, and the Word was God.'* (Jn 1:1)

"I love the idea of a religion that is based on love, which is best summed up in the quotation from St Paul, *'To live through love in God's presence.'* Every day I open the papers and I read stories about the absence of love in the world and it depresses me.

"Love of God is expressed not only in prayer and Sunday worship, but must permeate every aspect of our lives. The Bible has no ambiguities on one issue: you cannot love God unless you love your neighbour. The Old Testament prophets were scathing in their criticism of those who sought to appease God by prayers and sacrifices while oppressing the powerless. Jesus told us that all the law and the prophets are summarised in the commandment to love God and the neighbour. No words are minced when we are told: *"Whoever claims to love God but hates his brother or sister is a liar."* (I Jn 4:20) All love invites love. God calls us to love.

"I am enthralled by the compassion of God and Jesus to people. I'm always inspired by the image of Jesus in the Gospels. He was someone who brought the compassion of God to people, someone who didn't judge or condemn. He was someone who was with people wherever they were, especially those who found themselves on the margins of society. That is why I really admire people like Mother Teresa, because of the work she did with people who are unable to help themselves.

"One of the things that really interests me is the nature of goodness. I think Mother Teresa best sums it up. If we want to know what goodness is, we don't need to give big sermons or read heavy tomes – we just need to recall her work.

"Her recognition of the importance of prayer was prophetic and particularly relevant to us today. 'That's only a contemplative order' is a phrase one sometimes hears today when people are talking about religious life. Apart from what it betrays about our understanding of religious life, it also says something about our attitude to prayer. It is as if prayer is on the periphery of the Christian life, instead of at the very centre. In the hustle and bustle of our everyday lives, it is often difficult to find the inner stillness to make space for God to speak to us. Much of prayer is the struggle to overcome our many distractions, to concentrate on the presence of God. Solitude is a fertile state of mind and spirit in which it is possible to concentrate on something for a long time and also to establish a relationship with whatever you are concentrating on. Mother Teresa knew the importance of spending time alone with God."

A Pilgrim's Progress

The first impression I had as I stepped off the boat after a short open boat journey across the lake was of an island that was a mixture of Alcatraz and an abandoned holiday camp. The sun was gleaming off the darkening waters of the lake, a haven of primitive splendour. The south-west wind rushed through the reeds. The sound of the rocks was a sad one, challenging and threatening. This roar in the background came from the constant surging of the water off the rocks and reefs like the roar of distant drums. Lough Derg or Saint Patrick's Purgatory, a lake in County Donegal and one of the loneliest places in the world.

The purpose of the journey was to sample the old ascetic rigours of prayer, fast and vigil. We went barefoot over the island's million stones, did without sleep for twenty-four hours, fasted for three days and recited countless prayers. The diet, or lack of it, of watery tea and unbuttered bread, sharpened the religious appetite. As pilgrims conducted their penitential rounds in bare feet, they underwent a stripping-down in spirit that brought them closer to their Maker.

Historically Lough Derg has been the Celtic equivalent of the desert. In the western world, deprived of the sandy open spaces of the Sahara, the Celtic monks sought the sea. In Biblical times the desert in Scripture was the place of the revelation of God. The elemental experience on Lough Derg was to help pilgrims on this road of faith to go through the desert as the place of struggle and purification.

Light, faint at first, had ripened into the bold yellow of an autumn morning. It was a clear Irish day, white clouds lazy in blue skies, a cool breeze, sunlight on the rolling hills. Although it was late autumn it was unseasonably fine, and spring-like. As the cloud shadows racing in the wind flew over my head, trailing ribbons of shade and brightness over the endless blues and brown, I felt an overwhelming sense of aesthetic pleasure, despite my fears for the future. Not for the first time I really appreciated the natural beauty of my environment, particularly the marshy land, with its enchanting blanket of purple heather and bog pools with the black waters rippling and the tufts of rushes bending and swaying in the eternal wind.

It was then that I met Ciara O'Toole from Tipperary who had a strong devotion to Mother Teresa:

"Our house was the traditional Irish Catholic home. Statues or pictures of the Blessed Virgin adorned every room of the house. Saying the rosary was part of the furniture of our lives. For all these reasons devotion to Mary the Mother of God was as important to my childhood as reading comics, playing football and watching *Wanderly Wagon* on the television. The Blessed Virgin Mary was a kind of indirect line to God, a spiritual insurance policy. There were many times I resented this imposed religiosity. My father took this devotion a step further by wearing a scapular around his neck. An annual family ritual was a visit to Knock on the fifteenth of August. So I suppose that as a young girl I heard a lot about Mother Teresa.

"To me she was a real hero – albeit a reluctant one.

In the final scene of the medieval epic *La Chanson de Roland* the great Christian hero Charlemagne sat exhausted in Aix, his battles with the Moors over. According to the poem, he was more than 900 years old. An angel wakened the old man from his sleep and told him to get up again and return to battle because the work would not be finished until the end of time. Charlemagne sighed: '*Dieu, si penuse est ma vie.*' (O God, how hard is my life.) The work of the hero remains unfinished but who will do it if not he? It is highly unlikely that Mother Teresa's reading material included *La Chanson de Roland* but she certainly would have been able to identify with the sentiment.

"We often use words very casually. What do we really mean, when we speak of love, truth or beauty? It is easy to say that other four-letter word, 'love', as thousands of pop songs and romantic novels have shown, but it is much more difficult to practise it.

"Mother Teresa knew that love is at the very heart of the Christian life. After all, as we find in the first letter of St John, love is even God's definition. Christians are not simply God's possessions, but in a sense God's partners in loving. Mother Teresa in her care for the most damaged showed us what part of that new kingdom is.

"She showed us that little things do mean a lot. God has showered us with gifts – none more so than when he sent his only Son. Those gifts come with a challenge.

Christianity is not about occasional gestures of charity but about going the second mile, about making choices which involve inconvenience, discomfort and pain.

"Christ told us that the Good News is love. He came with a promise: 'I come that you may have life and have it to the full.' (Jn 10:10) The birth of Jesus offered a new beginning to the world, a new way of life. Mother Teresa calls us again to take up Jesus's invitation to make a new beginning. The heart of this invitation is love because it is through love alone that we please God and our main challenge is to acquire it. The God of the scriptures is an impatient figure, hungry to transform us into worthy bearers of the name 'Christian'. Jesus came on earth to love and be loved. The Christian life is an exchange of love – the love we receive and the love we give for Christ. To walk the way of unconditional love is to accept an arduous task.

"She had a passionate love of God. It is only insofar as we develop the full range of our capacities for loving that we become transparent, more vividly carriers of God's love. St Augustine recognised this in his famous dictum: *'Thou hast made us for thyself, O God, and our hearts cannot rest until they rest in thee.'*

St John of the Cross put it beautifully:

My beloved is the mountains,
And lonely wooded valleys,
Strange islands

And resounding rivers,
The whistling of love-stirring breezes
The tranquil night
At the time of rising dawn,
Silent music,
Sounding solitude,
The supper that refreshes, and deepens love.

"Heroism is often the bastard child of intense sorrow or need. Prompted by love of God, Mother Teresa had got involved in nursing the most broken and damaged and was furiously tender to them. Her love is a lamp for our steps and a light for our eyes. Her legacy to us is to make us aware of the life that makes us live, the expectation of a new beginning, new birth and hope and the inexhaustible potential that is all around us.

"As a child, I learnt with sadness about Jesus: His life, His suffering and His death. It did not make any sense to me that He had to suffer for our sins and that His death on the cross somehow held meaning and hope for all of mankind. Now, after experiencing my own small suffering, I could identify more with the life and meaning of Jesus. I could identify with His longing to be heard, His frustrations, His aching for human company to watch with Him through a night of pain and anguish and how His love for innocent children made him a magnet for them. But mostly and mainly I finally understood why Jesus came to earth, and how His actions and death were for each and every one of us. To see ourselves as being separate from God and from each other is an illusion. We are all connected to one another and if someone performs an unkind act then it, too, has an effect on us all.

"At the end of my life I'd like to be able to say that somehow I brought the compassion of God to people. There are days when I'm very far away from this, but I'm always inspired by the image of Mother Teresa working with the poor.

"Like Abraham Lincoln she had a dream. She wanted to see a just society – one which respects and nurtures all its children equally; insists that people and their human needs are sacrosanct; ensures that its wealth and resources are distributed fairly and equally and guarantees basic human rights for all its people. Perhaps a dream, but, as Abraham Lincoln said, 'the probability that we may fail in the struggle ought not to deter us from the support of a cause we believe to be just'."

Sister of Mercy

Sister Mary Killeen has been described as Ireland's answer to Mother Teresa. It is not a comparison that sits comfortably with her. Yet it is an understandable analogy given the nature of her work. Her passion for the poor can be traced back to her childhood.

"I was born in Phibsboro and I was very much

influenced by the Vincentians who were a very vibrant force in the parish, and I was very impressed by their emphasis, which was to like St Vincent de Paul, on helping the poor.

"I went to Careysford Training College to train as a teacher after I left school and during teacher training I was based in the famous Goldenbridge Primary School and in Cork Street, very poor areas. We saw the work the Sisters were doing there with the children from broken homes or the children where the foster care system hadn't worked properly, and were very impressed by their care. I felt kind of drawn to that sort of life but at the same time I was half-thinking of marrying someone.

"During training-college I got very sick. A girl came back to college with hepatitis and passed it on to me. I remember asking myself as I was sick: how would I like to die? So I promised myself that if I got better I was going to do something worthwhile with my life. That sickness had a huge effect on me so I decided to become a Sister. I didn't really want to be a nun but I felt it was something I should try and if it didn't work out then I would do something else."

After eight or nine years teaching in Ireland Sister Mary found that her superiors in the Sisters of Mercy had a surprise in store for her.

"I was asked to go to Kenya. I wasn't that keen. My father had just died and obviously it was not a time I wanted to leave my mother to cope on her own because it was a particularly tough time for her. I wasn't happy but a Sister in Kenya had become sick and she was the principal of a big Catholic school and they needed someone to replace her. I told them I wasn't thrilled at the prospect so they told me to think and pray about it. The next thing I knew they were presenting me with a ticket and visa!

"It was a big culture shock to be so far away and have no one you knew well to talk to. At the time it was very expensive to phone home. There was also the problem of living in a very different culture. The first few months I was numb from it all. I arrived on a Thursday and on the Monday morning I was head teacher of a primary school of over a thousand children. I was just barely thirty years old. The people were very nice and after a few months I began to really like the place."

Surprisingly the changes in religious practices that Sister Mary was initially exposed to were not as pronounced as might have been expected.

"When I went to Kenya first I was dealing with the same sort of belief system that we have in Ireland, because the middle-class churches were all run in Nairobi by Irish missionaries, but later on I moved to the slums."

Sister Mary found herself in a tale of two cities.

"The city was divided by a river. On one side were the comfortable homes of the middle class and on the other were the slums. The poor started to cross the river and look for education. Our school was already crowded but I got places for a hundred of them. They didn't mix in well with the existing students. They had no money for lunches. They were very hungry. They had no books and couldn't afford fees. I decided that if I was to really respond to their needs I would have to move to the slums. I was really, really shocked by what I saw and it affected me greatly. I saw that these people were living in the most horrific conditions. It beggared belief really.

"They also had no churches. We talk about the Church being the Church of the poor and that would make you laugh really. Here was a city with a million people living in houses and all the churches were there for them. Yet a million people were also living in the shanty towns but there wasn't a single Church to be found. When I went to start an informal school in 1985, I built a hall where they could go to Mass on Sundays. When they went to Mass in the middle-class churches they were very poorly dressed and dusty so they felt there was no welcome for them there. I felt it was no longer something I could do to go the slums but something I should do."

In Kenya, rural to urban migration is responsible for the high unemployment and the increased development of slums on the outskirts of the city of Nairobi. The cost of education, housing and healthcare is rising. Many children have no alternative but to roam the streets, exposed to crime, violence, drugs and prostitution. Some 60,000 children (1 in 6 being HIV positive) roam the streets of Kenya's capital city.

The Mukuru Centre which Sister Mary founded provides primary education for over 4,000 street children, daily food of maize and beans for each child in the five schools, rehabilitation of new street children, residential home for over a hundred orphans, community development programmes, social work and outreach to the slums, health education, post-primary skills training, and also sets up small businesses. Under the leadership of Sister Mary, the project takes care of approximately 6,000 street children, providing them with food, clothes, education and basic healthcare. She desperately wants to build a centre that will teach them the skills that will increase their chances of securing employment and give them the opportunity to become self-reliant.

"Theirs is a lost childhood and their only hope is the opportunity to go to school. The Mukuru Promotion Centre, under our stewardship, endeavours to help people to grow and to recognise their potential and to offer the children in our care the opportunity to become self-respecting, self-reliant adults, capable of effecting positive change in society."

For Sister Mary, Mother Teresa remains a source of challenge:

"We are challenged by Mother Teresa, like our foundress Catherine MacAuley, to work alongside the poor and to empower them to live with dignity, satisfying their need for food, health care, clothing, housing and education. She reminds us always that the poor need help today not next week.

"We are all children of God. Some Churches are very middle class and they expel those who are ragged. We try to make sure that those with nothing get something. I see God as the father or mother of us all – a loving, compassionate God. Mother Teresa reminds us that our God challenges the comfortable and is a God who challenges each one of us to reach out to people in need and those on the margins as Jesus himself did."

Driven

In the late 1980s Arnold O'Byrne became one of the best-known faces on Irish television as the frontman for an advertising campaign for Opel cars. Then all his Christmases came at once when, as Managing Director of the Company, he made the decision to sign an exclusive sponsorship deal with the Irish soccer team. Enter Jack Charlton and the rest is history.

Although Arnold has had great good fortune in his life he has also had more than his fair share of tragedy – notably the death of his son, Ian, after just three days.

"We were living in England at the time. Ian Patrick (he was born on St Patrick's Day) was our fourth child. The pregnancy had gone fine and we had no indication anything was wrong. My wife came home with Ian after two days. There was the usual excitement but after being home just one hour my wife asked if we could get the doctor because she felt things weren't quite right with Ian. I tried to assure her that the hospital wouldn't have let them home if there was any kind of problem but she remained unconvinced. We got the midwife and she checked Ian and said everything was fine.

"One thing I have learned throughout my life is that you should always trust a mother's instincts. My wife persisted and I rang the doctor very early the next morning. After he examined Ian he said that our little boy was probably brain-damaged and that he felt he should take Ian to the hospital to save time. After a short while we learned we had lost our child. I don't like the word 'lost'. He died.

"I remember it was a Friday. Why do I remember that? I don't know. I also remember going into the bedroom and holding my wife's hand. When our oldest girl, Audrey, who was five years old at the time came from school we had to tell her that Ian was gone to Heaven. I'll never forget her asking us, 'Why did it have to be my brother?'

"I went into the hospital that evening to complete

all the formalities. They suggested that I shouldn't see Ian because I should remember him alive and to this day I often question that advice. I walked home that evening. It was a two-mile walk. I cried the whole way home. I didn't think it was a manly thing to do. Now I feel that it is a manly thing to express your emotions.

"My wife was still in bed for the funeral so I went with my late mother-in-law. After a short ceremony at our church, St Joseph's, we proceeded to the graveyard. I carried Ian in his little white coffin and we buried him under a yew tree. His death probably had a bigger impact on me than I thought it would have. We thought we were over it but a few months later we went home to Ireland and we saw a nephew who was born at the same time as Ian. My wife cried her eyes out. So you wonder if you ever really get over it. We had two children after that but there was always a fear as the back of the mind that we might lose them."

Ian's death was not the only tragedy that darkened Arnold's life.

"I had an older brother, Sam. He was the sort of wonderful brother you read about in books. I can still think back to one Saturday afternoon when I was only seven and playing speedway on my bike and one of the pedals of the other lads' bike got caught in the spokes of my wheel and it was completely mangled. I was terrified of what my father was going to say to me. Sam was ten years older than me and was working as an apprentice carpenter. He brought it up to Balfe's bicycle shop in Irishtown and had the wheel repaired before Dad found out. Sam was on very low wages at the time so it was a huge sacrifice on his part.

"Years later when we were in England I got a phone call late one night. As I went to the phone I was certain in my mind that it was Sam calling me to tell me that either my mother or father had died. Instead it was Sam's father-in-law ringing me to tell that Sam had died suddenly. He was 37. You shouldn't die at 37. He left a wonderful wife and four children. His youngest child's third birthday was the following day. It had a devastating impact on me."

The suffering in his own life has equipped Arnold to reflect deeply on many issues in life. Not surprisingly when he was asked about his thoughts on Mother Teresa, Arnold produces a characteristically thoughtful response:

"I decided to put down on paper what little I knew about her and to reflect on some of those words.

"I knew she was born in Skopje, at that time part of Albania. I know little of Albania other than it was formerly a communist country and it is rife with tribal unrest. I can recall at the time of her death being surprised at her country of birth. Now I question the cause of that surprise. I know no Albanians but I suspect I had some negative preconceptions of a poor country and an uneducated people. I found myself questioning my preconceptions. Why should I be surprised at her place of birth? Who was I, in ignorance, to express such surprise? I reminded myself that no one can be judged on their birth country. We are born equal in the sight of God. I never questioned the birth place of Jesus.

"She was serene. The words I had originally written down were peace, calm, pious, but as I reflect I am of the opinion that 'serene' embraces those words. A serenity born of the knowledge that she was doing real work helping, in many different ways, to make the world a better place for so many.

"She was humble. I suspect material possessions mattered little to her. In meeting world leaders, dressed in her religious habit of blue and white, she was impressive in her humility and focused in her needs. I doubt if the wall of her room was adorned with photographs of such meetings or of awards given. Why bother with such things which are moments of life on this earth but matter little in the next life?

"She was committed. Commitment over a lifetime to any one cause is unusual. Too often commitment is given for short periods and in energetic bursts but all too soon to fade when the next cause is more popular. Over a sixty-year period she gave herself unstintingly to one cause, trying to alleviate the sufferings of so many and in so many different places. She built a caring organisation that she knew would continue her work when she died. That is real commitment.

"In just listing and reflecting on the above I have become more aware of my own failings and my own frailties. Perhaps Blessed Mother Teresa has expanded her horizons."

All in the Game

In the glory days of Jack Charlton's reign as Irish soccer manager one of the best-known faces on Irish television was the team's physio, Mick Byrne. Mick is the archetypal Dub.

"I was born and raised in the Inner City, in City Quay. My two aunties, Lord have mercy on them, worked in the chapel so I was very attached to it from a very early age. I used to help them clean the church, cut the grass for the priest and went in for meals with them. My favourite thing of all was to ring the Angelus bell.

"Religion at the time was everything. You were always scared of it back then. Looking back now there were no reasons for it but you were always threatened with being brought to the priest if you did anything wrong. Nothing happened of course. I also used to go to the Sodalities.

"I was an altar boy but we were banished from the

John Scally

altar during the Missions while the priest was giving his sermon in case we heard anything we shouldn't."

Although much of the religious practices of Mick Byrne's childhood are no longer fashionable he retains a deep love for one key element of Christian liturgy:

"I would really walk miles to get Mass on a Sunday. I have this thing that whatever country I am in, and I have been to a lot of them with the Irish soccer team, I would get Mass or make sure that Mass is said. One phrase that always stuck in my mind was something that my mother always said, 'The devil loves a Mass misser.' This will always be a part of me and I will never give it up. I love going to Mass. I don't portray myself as a religious freak because I was always my own man but I know the importance of looking for religion and of looking for guidance from God. I pray to God and the Blessed Virgin and St Anthony who is my saint. Any problems I've ever had I always pray to St Anthony.

"There were crossroads in my life and I brought them to God to help me find the right path. I've had to make difficult decisions so I prayed for guidance and those decisions were always right."

Yet Mick's prayers are never for purely selfish reasons.

"I pray for my children that they are successful in their work, in their study. One of my girls is away in Tenerife working as a teacher and I pray for her every day, that everything will go well for her, that she'll be healthy and that she'll be happy, and the same for my other children and my grandchildren. Everybody is included in my prayers that things will go right for them – if it's God's will and only if it's God's will. I always believe that if he wants me to have it I will get it because it is God's will.

"It's not easy to do at times, especially in times of sickness and death. I'm very much thinking now of when my mother and sister died. God was very much with me in those times, in my hours of need. I try and block that part out of my mind, which some people tell me is wrong. I haven't gone to see my mother's grave since she died because I can't bear to think of her dead. The same with my sister. They died within a few months of each other and that was a terrible time in my life. It's strange that I am really uncomfortable when I think of them dead but I have absolutely no fear of dying myself. I'm ready when He calls me any time. Mind you, I hope it won't be for a few years yet!"

It is hardly surprising, against that background, that Mick was a big admirer of Mother Teresa:

"She was a great woman, a remarkable woman. Her life had a value beyond compare, a value that she could not measure, which only time and eternity will reveal fully – a value in not what she could or could not do but, more importantly, in what and who she was. People saw her as one of God's special creatures and in her simplicity and vulnerability they discovered that people came first and that much happiness can be found in making time for each other."

An Officer and a Gentleman

The late Dermot Earley was one of the greatest footballers Roscommon has ever produced. In June 2007 he became Chief of the Staff of the Irish defence forces. He retired in June 2010. He brought a very clear philosophy to the job:

"In the late 1960's some of the students in my old school, St Nathy's College, Ballaghaderreen, gave a bit of a hiding to some younger pupils. As he sought to resolve the disciplinary issues, the Dean of Studies Father James Gavigan remarked: 'If you want to know what a person is like give them authority.' I have learned that attitude is more than ability, that the motives you have are more important than brains; the courage you have is much more important than all the ingenuity you can gather and that the most important thing of all is that your heart is in the right place.

"The late Oscar Traynor when he was Minister for Defence was invited to speak at the commissioning service for the new army officers. Given the tradition of long speeches everyone was surprised that his speech consisted of just four sentences: 'Congratulations on receiving your commission from the President. I understand you have a week off – enjoy it. You have now got weight – pull it. Don't throw it around." Those last two remarks enunciated a very helpful philosophy for someone taking on a challenging leadership role. It certainly resonates with my prejudices. Mother Teresa was somebody who by the force of her conviction and the force of her actions commanded authority, had her heart in the right place and offered leadership to the world and for these reasons and many others she will always have my respect and admiration."

John O'Mahony is one of the most respected GAA managers of all time having tasted success with Mayo, Leitrim and Galway. But there is more to John O'Mahony than just football. A former seminarian in Maynooth, Catholicism like the GAA was a formative influence of his youth. Hence it is little surprise that he too was a keen admirer of the former student in Rathfarnham:

"Mother Teresa of Calcutta was often pictured with a small baby in her arms and that is how I mostly visualise her. She entered the Loreto Order but later felt a deep calling to serve God by looking after His poorest people. She sought and got permission to found an order which would serve the poorest of the poor not just in India but in other countries. The nuns' simple habits and lifestyles are a reflection of the lifestyle of the poor amongst whom they live and serve. Mother Teresa's philosophy was that every human being is important to God and she made it her mission to rescue abandoned babies and children from the slums in Calcutta. Her Sisters came to live and work in Belfast at the height of the Troubles and they are still to be found serving the poorest of the poor in many corners of the world. The order is still attracting a large number of women willing to dedicate their lives to serving the poorest of the poor. Mother Teresa's philosophy of the need for care for all of God's people is in stark contrast to the materialistic and self-centred philosophy which is endemic in most Western societies. I firmly believe that it behoves all of us to aspire to Mother Teresa's set of values."

Another Irish sport-star was a big admirer of Mother Teresa. Tony Ward was one of the all-time great Irish rugby players:

"When I was younger I often wondered why there were so many poor people in the world when there seemed to be so much wealth all around. One answer might be that our political system, even our constitution, does not adequately protect the helpless, certainly if they are less than visible. And that prompts the most likely explanation of all. The reticence with which the issue of poverty has been approached does not help. When people have no voice, silence is not always golden.

"Mother Teresa sought to bring the bare necessities to

these people and their children and she knew that the greatest gift anyone could give these people is the gift of their time. She understood that a little goes a long way to a really poor people. She was someone who brought the compassion of God to people, someone who didn't judge or condemn. She was someone who was with people wherever they were, especially those who found themselves on the margins of society. Many people are good talkers. Mother Teresa talked by her actions."

Teen Idol

Maggie Burns is a young mother and baby masseur. Mother Teresa has been a constant presence in her life:

"When I think about Mother Teresa I am transported back to being a child. I grew up in a parish named St Thérèse and attended the adjoining national school of the same name. From a very early age I became fascinated with the lives of both Mother Teresa and St Thérèse of Lisieux (both were considered saints by our parish, one historic and one living saint, a concept I was charmed by). I believe the inspiration for Mother Teresa's religious name came from St Thérèse. Both life stories resonated with me as a small child because of the simplicity of their message, namely, to do unselfish acts of love. Mother Teresa spoke of the

Simple Path, how we could find God's love by loving others. St Thérèse called it 'The Little Way', a way of pleasing God by doing everything to the best of your ability and with a loving heart. All of this echoed the song we learnt in school, 'Make me a channel of your peace', another calling to give of yourself fully and not to count the cost.

"Back then it seemed to be easy, and that in doing things as well as I could and with as much love as possible, I could make a difference. I remember trying so hard to keep my bedroom tidy, or bringing up breakfast in bed to my mother and hoping that these small offerings would please God and somehow make the world a better place.

"Perhaps Mother Teresa with her small stature and innocent face was particularly appealing to me as a child, I imagined that I could talk to her and that she would be interested in me. I liked her thinking and remember seeing her on *The Late Late Show*. Her face was so familiar from posters in school and calendars at home that it felt as though Gay Byrne was interviewing an old friend. And yet the image of a frail child-like woman doesn't really fit – she must have been quite a gutsy woman to take on the work she did and to have overseen what became a very big project.

"Reflecting on Mother Teresa and St Thérèse of Lisieux, while there are many similarities there are also some differences. It seems that St Thérèse really wanted to be a saint, she devoted her whole life to pleasing God and offering up her work to God. Whereas when it was put to Mother Teresa that she was a 'living saint' she shrugged it off and said that she was just doing God's work, and constantly called her work simple and ordinary. Both entered religious life early, but while St Thérèse died very young – she was only twenty-four – Mother Teresa lived on to be eighty-seven.

"Mother Teresa most definitely inspired a youthful idealism in me. As a child and teenager I too shared her desire to make a difference in the world, to give my life meaning and to reach out to others. Some people pour that kind of energy into political activism, I wanted to be like Teresa and be a channel for God's love in the world. But when the youth went out of my youthful idealism, I waned in my desire to be good to others, and chose instead to be good to myself. I suppose this is not unusual where youth and idealism are concerned, but it seems that Mother Teresa kept that youthful zeal right up to the end of her long life. The magnitude of the work she took on is overwhelming even to imagine and she must have come up against many barriers which would have caused someone of lesser conviction to give up. Her faith and belief that she was doing what God wanted must have been tremendous to have carried her through the challenges she faced.

"Mother Teresa was, for me, the embodiment of

humanitarianism. Whenever I hear of aid projects and appeals around the world it feels like an extension of the work she took on in Calcutta. I think whenever I act charitably or extend myself beyond my comfort zone into a Christian outreach, my motivation still comes from the little girl inside who learnt the message of Mother Teresa in school.

"Not so long ago, I bought a tapestry for my daughter's room which reads: *'In this life we cannot do great things, we can only do small things with great love.'* I thought it was sweet and nothing more. It is only now that it has dawned on me that those were the words of Mother Teresa, and it has warmed my heart to realise that. I still live in the parish of St Thérèse and my children now attend the adjoining school, I wonder if the message of Mother Teresa will still be instilled in them as deeply as it was in me?

"The Catholic Church is in such a deep state of crisis right now, there has been so much hurt and so many lies. I think the only way back to its people is to be like Mother Teresa, to come away from hierarchies and power and instead revert to a simple Christianity where we love our neighbour as ourselves. To conclude I will borrow from Mother Teresa: *'If we have no peace, it is because we have forgotten that we belong to each other.'*"

Crossing the Religious Divide

As the son of a Church of Ireland clergyman, Philip McKinley is not the sort of a man who might be most easily associated with an interest in Mother Teresa but he is proof that she has an ecumenical appeal:

"In reflecting on the life and legacy of Blessed Mother Teresa, I am reminded of a story from ancient India, where there once was a king named Suddhodana who witnessed many horrors throughout his military career. When his son, Prince Siddhartha, was born he declared that the prince should be shielded from all knowledge of human suffering. The King built his son three luxurious palaces and surrounded him with only young, beautiful and healthy staff. However, when the Prince was twenty-nine years old, he ventured outside the palace and met for the first time in his life an old man, a diseased man and a decaying corpse. The Prince was so shaken and disturbed by the encounter that late one night, he escaped from his palace and abandoned his princely life to instead find meaning in the pains and sorrows of the real world.

"I don't know a great deal about Mother Teresa, no more than an average person I suspect. Most of my impressions revolve around the concept of Mother Teresa as a 'champion of the poor'. The only slight personal connection that springs to mind is from growing up in Rathfarnham in Dublin, where there was always a sense of local pride that Mother Teresa had been a member of the Loreto Order in Rathfarnham at the beginning of her ministry. I often wondered how her ministry formation in middle-class south Dublin equipped her for ministry in the poorest slums of Calcutta.

"However, I think the story of the Prince and his palace captures best my understanding of her. Even the mere mention of her name helps draw me out of my palace mentality, in whatever context that may be, into a world that is outside my comfort zone, yet is ultimately a place of profound discovery and personal transformation. It is for that reason that I think her legacy can have a private influence on some of the major challenges for us here in Ireland.

"My ecclesiastical identity is complex. I am a member of the Church of Ireland. I work however in two jobs, firstly part-time in a Methodist Church in West Dublin and also part-time as Dublin-based Ecumenical Officer with the Irish Inter-Church Committee. One great personal interest has been articulating, developing a contextual and practical social theology particularly amongst the minority Protestant traditions in the Republic of Ireland.

"The default position of any minority, whether social, cultural, economic, linguistic, religious etc is to 'look in'. Sociologists describe this as 'bonding', which is a very important process in the development of belonging, identity and social capacity. However, it is unhealthy for any community to remain at the 'bonding' stage – this can lead to a 'palace mentality'. Therefore every community should also develop ways of being a 'bridging' community as well. As Jesus says, we are called to be 'shepherds of sheep' as well as 'fishers of men'.

"For Protestants in the Republic, becoming a 'bridging' community has been a great challenge for a number of complex reasons. Theologically, Protestantism emphasises the individual more so than the community. Historically, the transition from Disestablishment to Irish Independence has been a traumatic one, as a church such as the Church of Ireland, once wealthy and all powerful, had to adjust to becoming a tiny, strange minority in just over a fifty-year period. One result from that time is that there are now too few people with too many churches having to therefore invest more in survival rather than service.

"Politically, socially and culturally, Protestants didn't fit in de Valera's de-colonising brand of Irish nationalism. Therefore to this day, Protestants are statistically less likely to be involved in community-orientated professions such as politics, the Garda or the army and are more likely to be involved in more enterprises such as farming or business. Finally, ecclesiastically, Irish Christian divisions are more pronounced and recognisable than probably any other country in the world, so a Protestant or Catholic in Ireland today can live an almost twin-track existence going to separate schools, playing separate sports, having separate nursing homes and being buried in separate graveyards.

"Social ministry is therefore difficult for any religious or confessional minority. However, Mother Teresa offers us a way of crossing these boundaries of class, ethnicity, denomination and religion, regardless of our history or status. She worked in the context of a deeply divided inter-religious society in India and, although a member of a tiny Christian minority, is today admired by Muslim, Hindu, Sikh and Buddhist alike for her single-mindedness, determination and bold prophetic action."

Philip is convinced that this tiny nun from Albania is still relevant for Irish people today:

"I believe Mother Teresa can also inspire us in our response to the profound changes in Irish Catholicism and indeed Irish Christianity. The day the Murphy Report was released, I checked my Facebook account and read with horror both the findings of the report which people were posting but also the vitriol of their response. These were people my age, twenty-eight, educated in Catholic schools, who identify themselves as Catholic and yet were posting comments about their Church which are simply unpublishable. The primary target of their anger was the Church's institutions.

"The German religious sociologist Max Weber makes an important distinction between concepts of 'institution' and 'charism'. He says that a 'charism' is a gift, purpose or ability from God that inspires and demonstrates Christian faith in an exceptional manner. However, 'charism' can only survive if it is given a human process, structure or institution. The human body for instance cannot survive without its skeleton. However, when you try and put charism in a box, you limit it, stifle it or even destroy it. This process he calls the 'routinisation of charism' and can only be overcome when charism is allowed to shape institutions rather than the other way around.

"Secularism is not totalitarian in its effect. Those Facebook comments represent not a militant atheism but rather an institutional Catholicism. Some commentators call this 'believing without belonging'.

"It's fascinating to note how another window of my culture, the Meteor Music Awards, Irish pop music's pinnacle showcase, indeed a temple of secularism and post-modernism, responds in a very different way to the Catholic Church. In the past seven years, three members of religious orders have been voted the recipients of the Meteor Humanitarian Award: Sr Stanislaus Kennedy, Fr Peter McVerry and Fr Shay Cullen.

"This perhaps shows that Christian charism rather than Christian institutions still hold the highest and deepest respect in society, especially among young people. Mother Teresa is testament to this. It is those that venture outside the palace into the grittiness, heartache and struggles of the world that still inspire. Mother Teresa's charism continues to motivate and challenge, transcending today's climate of anti-institutional Catholicism. Her ministry is perhaps therefore a sign of the green shoots of renewal and resurrection required in all institutional Churches today.

"I believe Mother Teresa has something profound to say to us in our current economic crisis. Indeed she may begin by telling us that when you compare the Irish economy to that of the Calcutta slums, we cannot call our situation a 'crisis'.

"I believe though that Mother Teresa may have seen a rich analogy between the Celtic Tiger and the palace existence of the prince. We built extensively, often with high security, unsustainable luxury and no regard for our imminent community or environment. We surrounded ourselves with beauty; it was the era of reality TV, celebrity culture and cosmetic surgery.

"We were a 'healthy' and confident nation, cured of our Famine baggage, now exporting our economic success, sporting success and cultural success through-out the world. It was suddenly cool to be Irish. We surrounded ourselves with 'youthfulness', living a Tír na nÓg lifestyle, in the here and now, on credit cards and dangerous bank loans. In 2006 Ireland was the second wealthiest OECD country in the world, based on average wealth. But when sickness, pain or death did occur, we were like the Prince, devoid of tools to con-ceptualise or respond adequately. We had lost a language of space in which to discuss the issues of ultimate importance. Our financial gain had blocked our access to a transcendent source of meaning. While the prince chose to leave the palace in search of the true meaning of life, we may feel as though we have been evicted involuntarily. Mother Teresa may still help us in our dismay to find new meaning in a world without wealth.

"I don't believe that Mother Teresa glorified poverty, but by simply living and working amongst the poorest in society, she inspired us to make sense of the world, not in the bright lights of the palace but in the shadows of the slum. So although Mother Teresa died over a decade ago, I believe her example and inspiration still provide direction and hope for us in our varied and complex struggles today."

A Constant Challenge

For Bishop Willie Walsh Mother Teresa has a critical message for the Irish Church today:

"The year 2009 will be seen in history as a year in which the Irish Church was in deep crisis. The Ryan and Murphy reports revealed an appalling litany of child abuse by priests and religious across the previous fifty years. It is too soon to judge how or whether the Church will recover from this crisis.

John Scally

"I believe that if we are to recover from this crisis our Church will have to examine how we departed so far from the gospel values of truth and justice, of compassion and love. We will need to examine how we can again put these values at the heart of our Church.

"Mother Teresa certainly can serve as an example of one who devoted her whole life and work to the values of compassion and love. Through her work for the poor she challenges us to return to gospel values given to us by the example and teaching of Jesus Christ. She can be a model, an inspiration and a challenge for all of us as we try to give new life and new meaning to our broken Church."

Chapter 9

The Last Word

After I turned off my tape-recorder and prepared to leave, Mother Teresa told me that one of her favourite stories was told to her during her time in Ireland. As I don't have her version, here is mine.

The abbot was distressed. He had woken up that morning early, long before the first faint vestiges of light illuminated the specklings of frost on the hard ground. As he pulled back the curtains the abbot was compelled to watch the world take shape despite his haste. The faint horizontal threads of clouds were growing a fiercer red against the still grey sky, the streaks intensified to scarlet and to orange and to gold, until the whole sky was a breath-taking symphony of colour. Sunrise so raised his spirits that the abbot could later easily understand why dawn worship had been a powerful primitive belief.

By now the monastery was swinging into action. It was a particularly busy day as for many people it was the time for the obligatory excursion to their Christmas confession for which many queued interminably.

Tradition also dictated that the day before Christmas Eve a great clean-up began and every room in the monastery was turned upside down and inside out as if very special visitors were coming. Everything was dusted, swept, scrubbed, scoured or polished, curtains were washed, and great piles of sticks were chopped and stored in the shed. On this day more than any other the abbot marvelled at the hand of God in the countryside.

He had always loved Christmas but this year was going to be a problem because he was going to have to hurt one of his monk's feelings. Some old customs could momentarily transfigure our existence and let the eternal shine through. One such custom was the singing of carols. They struck the abbot as simple ways of expressing those parts of Christianity that ordinary people found most interesting, not the parts that people ought to find most interesting. They were memorable because they were so tangible. They celebrated things that we could touch and see and warm to: a mother and a baby, though curiously not a father, or at least not a real father, a stable, donkeys, shepherds, straw and hay. Now though the singing of Christmas carols was causing him a major headache.

A few days ago his problem seemed resolved. The

problem had been dragging on now for a number of years. All the monks were getting very old and although they were still able to do their chores, their voices were well past their best and the community singing had suffered terribly. The main problem was of course, Brother Seán, who sang, if such a word could be used, in a high-pitched squeaky voice, doing violence to the ears of those unlucky enough to be in his immediate vicinity. Then, one day, as if by a miracle, a young man joined the community who had the voice of an angel. When he sang solo, everyone was enthralled by the sheer beauty of his voice; time just seemed to stand still. His solo singing brought a dramatic improvement to community worship, but not even he could cover up for Brother Seán.

Now the abbot faced a new problem. The local bishop had unexpectedly sent a message to say he would be starting a three-day visit to the community over Christmas. How could the abbot possibly subject the bishop to Brother Sean's singing? There was only one course of action: the abbot decided to instruct Brother Seán not to sing while the bishop was visiting. The abbot didn't want to hurt Brother Seán's feelings, but pleasing the bishop was more important than the pride of a simple monk.

Before Midnight Mass on Christmas Eve the abbot went out for a walk to clear his head and compose his thoughts for his sermon. Having the bishop attend added to the enormity of the occasion. He wriggled his toes and rubbed his gloveless hands to keep warm in the cold of early night. The stars were like holes in God's carpet which allowed the eternal light to shine through. He tiptoed in his shiny Wellingtons, avoiding heaps of cow dung in the stable. A hoar frost lay on the fields and the hedgerows were hung with the lace trimmings of what seemed to be a thousand spiders' webs. The monks' cattle were huddling under creeping hedges, staring vacantly up at the slate-grey sky with their stoic eyes, as they churned the day's grass.

When he went back inside a pang of guilt came back to him when he saw poor Brother Seán sitting quietly in the back of the chapel. Once Mass started though his conscience eased as the singing went beautifully. The abbot wore his best gold and white embroidered vestments, and the pale wax candles on the altar gleamed amid the lilies. On the window-ledges huge, white candles flickered slightly as a draught touched them, then shone as brightly as before. The smell of incense smelt more beautiful than a springtime primrose. The pungent scent of greenery mingled with the waxy smell of burning candles. The final candle in the advent wreath was then lit ceremoniously. So many of the abbot's images of Christ were etched in light, the silver of frost and moonlight, the shining Star of Bethlehem guarding the Magi and the radiance of the lighted candles.

Then came a solo rendering of "O Holy Night" that was so beautiful it worked a minor miracle and